AI Ready

Scale Your Organization's Generative AI Transformation Tomorrow With This No-Nonsense Guide Today

Tony Fatouros

© Copyright 2024 - All rights reserved.

The content contained within this book may not be reproduced, duplicated or transmitted without direct written permission from the author or the publisher.

Under no circumstances will any blame or legal responsibility be held against the publisher, or author, for any damages, reparation, or monetary loss due to the information contained within this book, either directly or indirectly.

Legal Notice:

This book is copyright protected. It is only for personal use. You cannot amend, distribute, sell, use, quote or paraphrase any part, or the content within this book, without the consent of the author or publisher.

Disclaimer Notice:

Please note the information contained within this document is for educational and entertainment purposes only. All effort has been executed to present accurate, up to date, reliable, complete information. No warranties of any kind are declared or implied. Readers acknowledge that the author is not engaged in the rendering of legal, financial, medical or professional advice. The content within this book has been derived from various sources. Please consult a licensed professional before attempting any techniques outlined in this book.

By reading this document, the reader agrees that under no circumstances is the author responsible for any losses, direct or indirect, that are incurred as a result of the use of the information contained within this document, including, but not limited to, errors, omissions, or inaccuracies.

Table of Contents

Preface

Your Role as a Change Leader in the Era of Generative AI

Generative Artificial Intelligence (GenAI) is not just an emerging technology; it's a revolutionary force reshaping industries, workflows, and business paradigms. As a leader, navigating this transformation isn't just about understanding new tools—it's about leading a fundamental shift in thinking and working assuming the role of a change leader.

This guide is crafted for leaders like you, who are prepared to steer their organizations through the dynamic landscape of GenAI. By embracing the role of a Change Leader, you will be at the forefront of this evolution, ensuring a seamless and impactful integration of GenAI into your operations.

Depending on your role, you might approach GenAI from various perspectives:

Managers: Champions of Implementing and Incorporating GenAI Initiatives

- **Change Management Practitioners:** Your mission is to gauge organizational readiness and craft change management strategies that prioritize the human aspects of GenAI adoption, such as training, culture, and stakeholder engagement.

- **Project Managers:** Your role is to delineate and oversee the implementation activities for GenAI initiatives.

- **IT Managers:** You need to comprehend and tackle the changes that GenAI introduces into technology operations.

- **HR Practitioners:** You will evaluate the implications for employees in Learning and Development, Job, and Organizational Design.

- **Business Leaders:** Your focus is on leveraging GenAI opportunities to bridge the gap between technology and business outcomes, thereby enhancing processes, customer experiences, and driving revenue growth.

Executives: Visionaries Scaling GenAI Opportunities Across the Organization

- **CxOs:** You are responsible for steering your organization through the strategic and ethical dimensions of GenAI, ensuring alignment with the overarching vision and goals.

- **Technology Executives:** You drive innovation by identifying and integrating GenAI technologies, pivotal in unlocking its technical potential and applications.

- **Transformation Executives:** You develop and spearhead comprehensive roadmaps for GenAI integration, leading the charge into new operational paradigms and exploring novel business opportunities.

- **HR Leaders:** You address the workforce implications of GenAI, orchestrating reskilling and upskilling initiatives, and adapting talent strategies to cultivate an AI-ready culture.

- **Legal and Compliance Executives:** You navigate the organizational risks associated with rapidly evolving laws and uses related to GenAI.

Change is a collective endeavor, requiring leaders from diverse areas to collaborate and take a holistic approach. This transition is not just about adopting new technology; it's about redefining our approach to work and thought. Regardless of your organizational role, you are an integral part of this transformation.

How Change Leaders Should Use This Guide

A few years ago, while working for a global consumer electronics company, I experienced firsthand the critical importance of aligning people, processes, and technology. Our team was tasked with implementing new systems and processes to support direct-to-consumer shipping. The systems were meticulously built, and the team was thoroughly trained. However, due to poorly documented and misunderstood shipping procedures, the initiative ultimately failed. The result was an inconsistent customer experience that undermined the entire program.

This experience underscored a vital lesson: successful organizational change hinges on the alignment of people, processes, and technology. We call this alignment "Organizational Readiness."

Organizational Readiness: The Core of This Guide

The primary focus of this guide is "Organizational Readiness," a cornerstone for successfully scaling Generative AI to drive growth and competitive advantage. To make this tangible and actionable, we've broken it down into three main areas:

1. **Governance:** Establishing clear policies, ethical guidelines, and oversight mechanisms.

2. **Technology:** Integrating GenAI technologies seamlessly into existing systems and operations.

3. **Workplace:** Ensuring your workforce is prepared, reskilled, and aligned with the new ways of working introduced by GenAI.

Each of these areas will be explored in detail, providing you with the tools and insights needed to navigate and lead this transformative journey.

For example, the Governance category can be broken down into the following components:

1. **Policy and Compliance:** Establishing and enforcing organizational policies.

2. **Decision-Making Structures:** Defining roles and responsibilities for decision-making.

3. **Risk Management:** Identifying and mitigating potential risks.

4. **Transparency and Accountability:** Ensuring open communication and holding individuals accountable.

Our goal is to equip you with a comprehensive roadmap for aligning people, processes, and technology, ensuring that your organization is not only ready to adopt GenAI but also poised to leverage it for sustainable success.

The GenAI Organizational Readiness Model, which will be introduced shortly, encapsulates all these concepts.

By the end of this guide, Change Leaders will be equipped to evaluate their organization's readiness and create a detailed roadmap with key milestones to facilitate GenAI adoption.

As AI becomes increasingly integral to your organization, the prompt introduction and development of these components are crucial. Understanding their importance, implementing them correctly, and recognizing the potential consequences of their absence are essential steps. This insight is vital for accelerating your organization's preparedness to embrace and benefit from AI advancements.

Let's embark on this journey together, confidently ready to face the future.

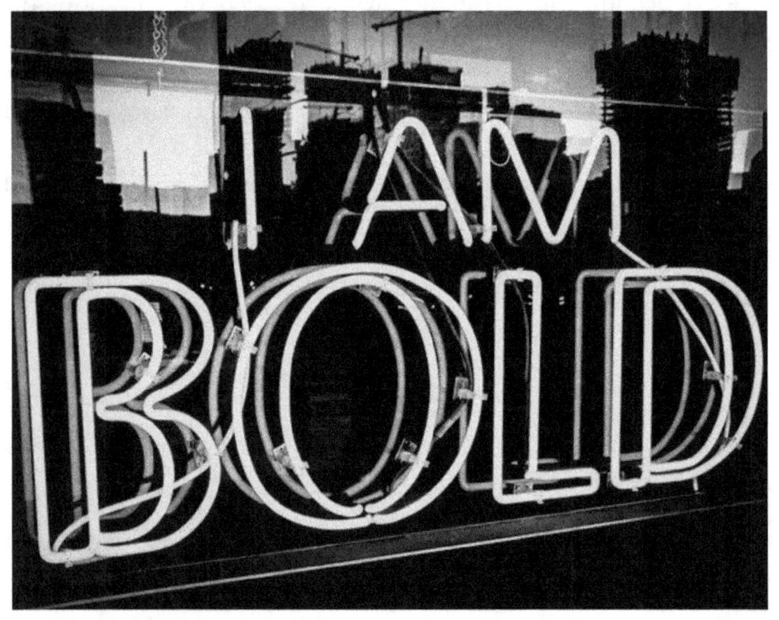
I AM
BOLD

Introduction

The Increasing Need for GenAI-Informed Leaders

In 2023, Generative AI experienced a significant leap forward, marking a pivotal moment in its adoption across various sectors. The technology's rapid advancement was epitomized by ChatGPT, developed by OpenAI, which reached an astounding 100 million users by January 2023—just 2 months after its launch. This milestone underscored the burgeoning interest and potential that AI technologies hold for the future.

Initially, organizations approached Generative AI cautiously. They embarked on small-scale projects to explore its capabilities and understand its boundaries. These pilot projects were often concentrated in areas like content creation, customer support, and data analysis. The goal was to gauge the technology's effectiveness and identify potential pitfalls before committing to broader implementation.

As the year unfolded, these experimental projects began to scale. Companies started integrating Generative AI into their core operations, recognizing its value in augmenting various business functions. In the realm of marketing, AI-generated content provided a new avenue for creativity and efficiency, while in customer service, AI chatbots grew increasingly adept at managing diverse and complex inquiries. This shift toward larger-scale applications signaled a deepening trust in AI's capabilities.

Major technology companies such as Microsoft, Salesforce, and Zoom were at the forefront of this integration. They swiftly incorporated Generative AI into their products and services, enhancing them with innovative AI-driven solutions. By 2024, these enhancements had become more sophisticated and widely available, demonstrating the transformative impact of AI on the tech landscape.

However, the widespread adoption of Generative AI was not without its challenges. One major hurdle was ensuring the accuracy and quality of AI-generated content. This concern prompted organizations to develop robust oversight and quality control processes. Additionally, ethical considerations came to the fore, particularly regarding the potential for AI to produce biased or inappropriate content. Addressing these issues became paramount to maintaining the integrity and trustworthiness of AI applications.

Upskilling the workforce to collaborate effectively with AI tools emerged as another critical focus area. Organizations recognized the need for comprehensive training programs that would equip employees with the necessary skills and foster a mindset shift. Viewing AI as a collaborative tool rather than a replacement was essential to harnessing its full potential.

Investment in AI technology surged, reflecting the growing confidence in its potential. According to Crunchbase (Teare, 2024), investment in AI technology startups surpassed $27 billion, with analysts predicting even greater investment in the coming years. This influx of capital underscored the high stakes and immense opportunities associated with AI technology.

Today, Generative AI has become an integral component of many organizations' digital transformation strategies. Its applications have grown more sophisticated, and its integration into business processes has become more seamless. Companies continue to explore and expand AI use, driven by the promise of innovation, efficiency, and competitive advantage.

Effective change management has emerged as a crucial factor in ensuring a smooth transition as organizations integrate new AI technologies. The path to successful AI adoption is fraught with potential challenges and resistance to new ways of working. A critical component of change management is organizational readiness—preparing the workforce and infrastructure to embrace and leverage AI tools.

This guide was developed to assist leaders in identifying the types of GenAI initiatives they may be supporting. It aims to help them recognize the mechanisms organizations will need to successfully adopt Generative AI. By providing a roadmap for navigating the complexities of AI integration, this guide empowers leaders to drive sustainable and impactful transformation within their organizations.

GenAI Organizational Readiness Model

CATEGORY	COMPONENT	Proof of Concept (Experiments)	Quick Wins (Employee Tasks)	Changes (Single Department Processes)	Cross Functional (Multi-Department Processes)	Transformational (New Business)
GOVERNANCE	Steering Leadership	●	●	●	●	●
	Ethics & Responsible Use	●	●	●	●	●
	Legal	●	●	●	●	●
	Usage		●	●	●	●
TECHNOLOGY	Data	●	●	●	●	●
	Architecture	●	●	●	●	●
	Security	●	●	●	●	●
	Vendor Standards	●	●	●	●	●
	IT Maturity				●	●
WORKFORCE	Training	●	●	●	●	●
	Organizational Point of View		●	●	●	●
	Culture		●	●	●	●
	Roles		●	●	●	●
	Talent Management			●	●	●

CHANGE COMPLEXITY & RISK →

The GenAI Organizational Readiness Model has been meticulously developed using best practices derived from extensive company experiences, insights from change management, technological advancements, and in-depth discussions with technology and industry leaders. This model serves as a vital tool for organizations looking to embark on AI initiatives, providing a structured framework to evaluate and enhance their readiness.

In an era where artificial intelligence is rapidly transforming the business landscape, organizations are constantly seeking ways to stay ahead of the curve. However, the journey toward successful AI integration is fraught with complexities, uncertainties, and risks. This is where the GenAI Organizational Readiness Model becomes indispensable.

Imagine having a comprehensive guide that not only highlights the critical components your organization needs to focus on but also categorizes AI initiatives based on their complexity and risk. This model does just that, encompassing insights from the frontlines of industry innovation, change management strategies, and the collective wisdom of top-tier executives.

Why This Model Is a Game-Changer

- **Real-World Experience:** The model is grounded in practical experiences from numerous organizations that have successfully navigated the AI landscape. By learning from their journeys, your organization can avoid common pitfalls and leverage proven strategies.

- **Holistic Approach:** It integrates change management principles and technological advancements, ensuring that every aspect of organizational readiness is covered. Whether it's governance, technology, or workplace culture, this model provides a 360-degree view.

- **Expert Insights:** Developed in collaboration with technology and industry leaders, the model encapsulates the nuanced understanding and forward-thinking perspectives of those at the helm of technological innovation.

- **Strategic Roadmap:** Serving as a strategic roadmap, the model helps leaders anticipate challenges and complexities. It enables proactive planning and effective management of the change process, ensuring that AI initiatives are not only launched but also sustained and scaled successfully.

As you dive into this model, you'll discover a matrix that outlines the relationship between organizational readiness components and different types of AI initiatives. The matrix is divided into three main categories—Governance, Technology, and Workplace—each representing a crucial aspect of organizational readiness.

Adjacent to these categories are five types of AI initiatives, ranging from simple Proof of Concepts to transformative new business ventures. Each dot in the matrix represents a specific readiness component necessary for the successful implementation of an AI initiative.

At the bottom of the matrix, an arrow labeled "CHANGE COMPLEXITY AND RISK" signifies that as you move from left (Proof of Concept) to right (Transformational), the complexity and risk associated with the AI initiatives increase.

This model is not just a theoretical framework; it's a practical, actionable tool that can guide your organization through the multifaceted landscape of AI integration. By leveraging this model, you can turn potential challenges into opportunities and ensure that your AI initiatives drive significant business value.

Prepare to embark on a transformative journey with the GenAI Organizational Readiness Model.

Dream
Big

Part I:
The Organizational AI Journey

Organizations often start with Gen AI Proof of Concepts (PoC) before progressing to full business transformations, a practice that has emerged from the lessons learned during the early adoption of AI technologies. The history of this approach can be traced back to the experiences of pioneering organizations that embarked on their AI journeys in the early 2010s.

In the early days of AI adoption, many organizations rushed to implement AI solutions without fully understanding the technology's capabilities, limitations, and potential impact on their business processes. This eagerness to jump on the AI bandwagon often led to failed projects, wasted investments, and disappointment. A notable example is the case of MD Anderson Cancer Center, which made headlines in 2017 for its failed IBM Watson AI project. The project, which aimed to use AI to help doctors match patients with clinical trials, was abandoned after spending $62 million due to challenges in integrating the technology with the hospital's existing systems and processes (Bohr & Memarzadeh, 2020).

Learning from these early missteps, organizations began to recognize the importance of a more cautious and measured approach to AI adoption. The concept of starting with Proof of Concepts gained traction as a way to mitigate risks and validate the feasibility of AI solutions before committing significant resources. In 2018, Gartner predicted that by 2022, 85% of AI projects would deliver erroneous outcomes due to bias in data, algorithms, or the teams responsible for managing them (van der Meulen & McCall, 2018). This prediction highlighted the need for organizations to carefully evaluate and test AI solutions before deploying them at scale.

The success of early Gen AI PoCs, such as OpenAI's GPT-2 and Google's BERT, further reinforced the value of this approach. These PoCs demonstrated the potential of GenAI technologies in various domains, such as natural language processing, content generation, and sentiment analysis. Organizations across industries took notice and began to explore how they could leverage GenAI to enhance their operations and gain a competitive edge.

In 2019, the pharmaceutical company Novartis announced a PoC using Microsoft's AI technology to accelerate the discovery and development of new drugs (*Novartis and Microsoft announce collaboration to transform medicine with artificial intelligence*, 2019). These examples illustrate how organizations are using PoCs to validate the potential of GenAI in their specific contexts before embarking on larger-scale implementations.

As more organizations shared their experiences and best practices, the approach of starting with GenAI PoCs before progressing to full business transformations became a widely accepted practice. Industry leaders and experts advocated for this staged approach, emphasizing the importance of learning, iteration, and gradual scaling. In a 2021 document, McKinsey & Company recommended that organizations adopt a "test-and-learn" mindset when implementing AI, starting with small-scale pilots and gradually expanding to more complex use cases (*Global banking practice: Building the AI bank of the future*, 2021).

Today, starting with GenAI PoCs has become a standard practice for organizations looking to leverage the technology for business transformation. This approach allows organizations to explore the potential and limitations of GenAI in a controlled, low-risk environment, build confidence in the technology, and develop the necessary skills and capabilities before embarking on more ambitious initiatives. As the field of GenAI continues to evolve, organizations that adopt this staged approach will be better positioned to navigate the challenges and opportunities that lie ahead.

The Importance of a Staged Approach to GenAI Adoption

PoC projects serve as a foundational step, allowing organizations to explore and understand the potential and limitations of GenAI technologies in a controlled, low-risk environment. These initial experiments are crucial for validating the feasibility of AI solutions without the commitment of extensive resources or the risk of significant disruption. By starting with PoCs, organizations can test the waters and gain valuable insights into how GenAI can be leveraged to address specific business challenges or opportunities. This approach aligns with the best practices that have emerged from the early experiences of AI adoption, where rushing into full-scale implementations without proper validation often led to failed projects and wasted investments.

The controlled nature of PoCs allows organizations to evaluate the technical feasibility, data requirements, and potential benefits of GenAI solutions. By focusing on a narrow scope and well-defined objectives, PoCs provide a safe space for experimentation and learning. This hands-on experience helps decision-makers understand the practical implications of adopting GenAI and identify any gaps or challenges that need to be addressed before scaling up the initiatives. The insights gained from PoCs are invaluable in informing the organization's AI strategy and guiding future implementations.

As organizations gain confidence and knowledge from these PoCs, they gradually move towards more impactful implementations. The lessons learned from the PoCs serve as a foundation for the next steps, allowing organizations to refine their strategies and prioritize areas where GenAI can deliver the most value. Quick Wins, which focus on enhancing specific employee tasks, often follow PoCs, offering immediate benefits and further embedding AI into the organizational workflow. These Quick Wins demonstrate the tangible value of GenAI in a real-world setting and help build momentum and buy-in from employees.

By targeting specific employee tasks, Quick Wins showcase how GenAI can enhance productivity, streamline processes, and improve decision-making. The success of these initiatives reinforces the potential of GenAI and prepares the workforce for more significant changes down the line. As employees experience the benefits of AI firsthand, they become more receptive to broader implementations and are better equipped to adapt to the changes brought about by the technology.

This step-by-step progression from PoCs to Quick Wins and then to more complex GenAI initiatives ensures a smoother adoption of AI within the organization. It allows for a gradual introduction of AI capabilities, giving employees the opportunity to build trust in the technology and develop the necessary skills to leverage it effectively. This incremental approach also enables organizations to address any technical, data, or skills gaps identified during the PoCs and Quick Wins before embarking on larger-scale implementations.

Navigating the Path to GenAI Transformation

However, it's important to note that depending on the opportunities and readiness, some organizations may choose to launch directly from PoCs into more complex GenAI initiatives. This accelerated path may be suitable for organizations with a clear vision, strong technical capabilities, and a culture that embraces innovation and change. These organizations may have the resources and expertise to navigate the challenges of more ambitious AI projects and are willing to take on a higher level of risk in pursuit of transformative outcomes.

Regardless of the path taken, leaders play a crucial role in the successful implementation of AI projects. They are responsible for guiding the organization through the AI journey, aligning stakeholders, and managing the people side of change. Leaders must be attuned to the specific type of GenAI project they are supporting, as this guides the change management strategy and approach. By understanding the nature and scope of the GenAI project, leaders can develop targeted communication plans, training programs, and support mechanisms to ensure successful adoption and realization of benefits.

PoC projects serve as a foundational step in an organization's GenAI journey, allowing for controlled experimentation, risk mitigation, and validation of AI solutions. As organizations gain confidence and knowledge from these PoCs, they progress towards more impactful implementations, such as Quick Wins and more complex GenAI initiatives. This step-by-step approach, which has been informed by the lessons learned from early AI adopters, ensures a smoother adoption of AI and enables organizations to realize the full potential of the technology. Leaders play a vital role in guiding the organization through this journey, aligning stakeholders, and managing the people side of change to ensure successful outcomes.

Navigating the Landscape of GenAI Projects: Types, Complexities, and Risks

Let's explore the differences among the types of AI projects and associated risks in the following table:

Type of AI Project	Description	Change Management Complexity	Project Risks
Proof of Concept (Experiments)	PoC projects in AI are experimental endeavors exploring the potential of GenAI technologies. Typically, these are small-scale projects validating the feasibility and effectiveness of AI solutions in a controlled environment.	Limited in scope and impact, focusing on learning about AI capabilities. Lower readiness requirements but foundational.	Risks include underestimating resources needed, overestimating technology capabilities, and lack of integration with existing systems.

Continued on next page…

Type of AI Project	Description	Change Management Complexity	Project Risks
Quick Wins (Employee Tasks)	GenAI solutions to enhance specific employee tasks, like using ChatGPT for draft copywriting. Aims to streamline workflows and increase efficiency in targeted areas.	Requires focused training and user adoption as they directly affect daily tasks of employees.	Risks involve resistance to change, integration challenges with existing systems, and disruptions during transition.
Changes (Single Department Processes)	Implementing GenAI to transform processes within a single department, like chatbots in customer service. Enhances departmental efficiency.	Significantly alters workflows, requiring substantial training and adaptation from the department.	Risks include resistance from employees, disruptions to operations, and continuous adjustments for AI evolution.

Type of AI Project	Description	Change Management Complexity	Project Risks
Cross-Functional (Multi-Department Processes)	Broader scope projects impacting end-to-end processes across multiple departments, like AI-driven supply chain optimization.	Demands comprehensive change management encompassing multiple departments with varied needs.	Risks include misalignment between departments, complex integration issues, and potential for large-scale operational disruptions.
Transform-ational (New Business)	Projects that create new lines of business or capabilities, like entering music production in a book publishing business.	Requires a fundamental rethinking of business models, extensive training, and potentially a cultural shift within the organization.	Risks are substantial, including strategic misalignment, significant financial investment with uncertain returns, and managing extensive change.

Examples of each type of GenAI project are provided below to assist leaders in understanding their starting point for Organizational Readiness. By examining these examples, leaders can determine if any important considerations have been missed and anticipate what may lie ahead in their GenAI journey.

These examples span across various industries and business functions, showcasing the diverse applications of GenAI technologies. From Proof of Concept experiments to Transformational new business initiatives, these examples highlight the potential impact and challenges associated with each type of GenAI project.

Human Resources Example

Type of AI Project	**Human Resources**
Proof of Concept (Experiments)	**Initial Candidate Screening With GenAI** Develop a cutting-edge AI-powered tool that empowers HR teams to streamline the candidate screening process. By inputting candidate resumes, the tool leverages advanced natural language processing and machine learning algorithms to provide instant, data-driven insights on candidate suitability. The intelligent system analyzes resumes against predefined job requirements, identifying key skills, experience, and qualifications that align with the position. HR professionals can interactively adjust parameters, such as the relative importance of specific skills or experience, and receive real-time feedback on how these changes impact candidate rankings. This dynamic and user-friendly tool enables HR teams to make more informed decisions, reduces time spent on manual screening, and enhances the overall efficiency and effectiveness of the hiring

	process. By harnessing the power of GenAI, organizations can identify top talent quickly and objectively, ultimately leading to better hires and improved business outcomes.
Quick Wins (Employee Tasks)	**Creating Job Postings With ChatGPT** Introducing a GenAI solution that empowers HR professionals to create compelling and tailored job postings effortlessly. By simply inputting essential job details, users can leverage the power of AI to generate high-quality job descriptions. The interactive platform allows for seamless refinement, enabling HR teams to modify and add specific requirements or benefits with ease. As users make adjustments, the AI adapts the posting in real-time, ensuring it aligns perfectly with the company's unique tone and branding guidelines. This innovative tool streamlines the recruitment process, saving valuable time and resources while attracting top talent through engaging and personalized job postings.
Changes (Single Department Processes)	**Deploying an AI Chatbot for Handling Employee Queries in HR** Implementing a GenAI-driven chatbot that employees can interact with to get quick, accurate answers to common HR-related questions. The chatbot leverages natural

	language processing and machine learning to understand employee inquiries and provide personalized, real-time responses. It can handle a wide range of topics, including benefits, policies, procedures, and frequently asked questions. The AI chatbot acts as a first line of support, available 24/7 to address employee needs. For more complex or sensitive queries that require human judgment or expertise, the chatbot seamlessly escalates the conversation to a human HR representative. This hybrid approach combines the speed and convenience of AI with the empathy and problem-solving skills of human support. By automating responses to routine questions, the AI chatbot frees up HR staff to focus on higher-value activities like employee engagement, talent development, and strategic initiatives. It also improves the employee experience by providing instant, consistent answers and reducing wait times. Implementing an AI chatbot in HR is a powerful way to streamline support, boost efficiency, and enhance employee satisfaction.
Cross-Functional (Multi-Department Processes)	**Revolutionizing Recruitment With AI** Implementing a cutting-edge GenAI platform that seamlessly integrates with multiple departmental systems, including HR, IT, and hiring managers, to streamline the entire recruitment process. This innovative solution empowers hiring

	managers to input precise job requirements, enabling the AI to efficiently source high-quality candidates, schedule interviews, and generate comprehensive onboarding checklists. The interactive platform facilitates real-time updates and fosters effective collaboration across departments, ensuring a cohesive and efficient hiring experience. By leveraging the power of AI, organizations can significantly reduce time-to-hire, improve candidate quality, and enhance the overall recruitment process, ultimately leading to a more productive and engaged workforce.
Transformational (New Business)	**Creating an Industry-Specific Learning and Development Platform** Develop an AI-driven platform that tailors learning content to individual employee needs within a particular industry. The platform will feature an AI chatbot that interacts with employees, assessing their current skills, knowledge gaps, and career goals through engaging conversations. Based on this information, the chatbot will provide personalized training recommendations, suggesting relevant courses, webinars, and learning materials that align with the employee's needs and the industry's best practices. As employees progress through their learning paths, the chatbot will offer real-time support, answering questions, providing guidance, and offering encouragement. The AI will continuously adapt and refine the learning

	paths based on user feedback, performance data, and industry trends, ensuring that the development opportunities remain relevant and effective. This approach will create a dynamic and engaging learning experience that promotes continuous growth and skill acquisition, ultimately contributing to the success of both the employees and the organization within their specific industry.

Finance Example

Type of AI Project	**Finance**
Proof of Concept (Experiments)	**Testing an AI Tool for Financial Forecasting** Develop an AI-powered financial forecasting tool that utilizes machine learning algorithms to predict future financial performance for businesses. The tool will integrate with existing financial data sources, analyze historical data, market trends, and key performance indicators to generate accurate and timely forecasts. Users can interact with the AI through an intuitive interface, inputting assumptions and variables to explore various scenarios. The tool will provide visualizations, dashboards, and recommendations for optimizing financial strategies. By continuously learning and adapting based on new data and user feedback, the AI will ensure the accuracy and reliability of the

	forecasts, enabling businesses to make data-driven decisions, anticipate future financial performance, and proactively manage risks.
Quick Wins (Employee Tasks)	**Using Microsoft Copilot to Analyze Data in Excel** Leverage Microsoft Copilot, an AI-powered assistant, to streamline data analysis in Excel. With Copilot, users can input natural language queries, and the AI will automatically generate the appropriate formulas, functions, and visualizations to answer their questions. For example, users can ask Copilot to "calculate the average sales revenue for the past 12 months" or "create a pivot table showing the top 5 products by revenue." Copilot will then execute the necessary commands and present the results in a clear and actionable format. By learning from user interactions and feedback, Copilot will continuously improve its understanding of the user's needs and preferences, providing increasingly accurate and relevant insights over time. This AI-driven approach to data analysis in Excel will save users time, reduce errors, and empower them to make data-driven decisions more.
Changes (Single Department Processes)	**Using Generative AI for Automated Regulatory Compliance Reporting** Implementing a sophisticated Generative AI system to revolutionize the process of regulatory compliance reporting. This

	advanced system automatically extracts, analyzes, and summarizes critical information from vast and complex datasets, ensuring that the generated reports adhere to stringent regulatory standards. By leveraging AI, the reporting process becomes significantly more efficient, accurate, and timely, allowing financial institutions to maintain compliance effortlessly while freeing up valuable human resources for more strategic tasks.
Cross-Functional (Multi-Department Processes)	**End-to-End Financial Reporting Automation** Using Generative AI, organizations can revolutionize the entire process of financial report generation. This end-to-end automation begins with the collection of financial data from various sources, including internal databases, external feeds, and real-time transactions. GenAI algorithms then analyze this data, identifying trends, anomalies, and key performance indicators (KPIs) with unparalleled speed and accuracy. Following the analysis, GenAI can draft comprehensive financial reports tailored to specific needs and compliance requirements. These reports are not just collections of numbers; they include in-depth insights that are crucial for strategic decision-making. Chatbots driven by GenAI further enhance this process by

	offering dynamic interaction with the data, allowing users to query specific metrics or request additional explanations and visualizations in real time.
Transformational (New Business)	**Creating an AI-Driven Financial Advisory Service** Developing a new business line offering personalized investment and financial planning considerations generated by AI, tailored to individual customer profiles and preferences.

Marketing Example

Type of AI Project	**Marketing**
Proof of Concept (Experiments)	**Testing AI-Generated Ad Copy** Implementing GenAI to create and test different versions of ad copy for social media campaigns, analyzing engagement to determine effectiveness.
Quick Wins (Employee Tasks)	**Automating Email Marketing** Using GenAI to automatically generate personalized email content for various segments of the customer base, enhancing engagement and reducing manual effort.
Changes (Single Department	**Generating Personalized Product**

Processes)	**Recommendations** Deploying GenAI to create personalized product suggestions for users based on their browsing and purchase history, improving conversion rates and customer satisfaction.
Cross-Functional (Multi-Department Processes)	**End-to-End Campaign Automation** Using GenAI to automate the entire marketing campaign process, from content creation and scheduling to performance analysis and optimization across multiple channels.
Transformational (New Business)	**Creating AI-Driven Content Studios** Developing a new business line that uses GenAI to produce high-quality, personalized video content and graphics for clients at scale, transforming the content creation process and offering innovative services to customers.

Operations Example

Type of AI Project	Operations
Proof of Concept (Experiments)	**Testing GenAI for Interactive Predictive Maintenance** Implementing a GenAI tool that allows maintenance staff to input current

	equipment conditions and receive AI-generated predictions and recommendations for upcoming maintenance needs. The tool can interactively suggest the best times for maintenance based on historical data and real-time inputs from users.
Quick Wins (Employee Tasks)	**Automating Interactive Report Generation** Using GenAI to create operational reports where users can input specific data points or queries. The AI generates detailed reports based on these inputs, allowing employees to interactively refine the report's focus and content, ensuring the final output meets their exact needs.
Changes (Single Department Processes)	**Enhancing Warehouse Operations With GenAI-Generated Interactive Workflows** Deploying a GenAI system that employees can interact with to optimize picking routes and warehouse layout. Workers can input their daily tasks, and the AI provides real-time, optimized workflows and route suggestions, adapting to changes and feedback from the users throughout the day.
Cross-Functional (Multi-Department Processes)	**Optimizing Supply Chain Logistics With Interactive GenAI Simulations** Utilizing GenAI to create and simulate

	various logistics scenarios. Users from procurement, production, and distribution departments can input their parameters and constraints, and the AI generates optimized logistics plans. The interactive tool allows users to adjust variables and immediately see the impact on the overall logistics strategy.
Transformational (New Business)	**Creating an Interactive AI-Driven Customer Support System** Developing a new service that uses GenAI to provide personalized customer support. Customers can interact with the AI by asking questions or describing issues. The GenAI generates responses and solutions in real-time, offering a seamless, interactive support experience across multiple channels, including chat, email, and voice interfaces.

Research and Development Example

Type of AI Project	Research and Development
Proof of Concept (Experiments)	**Testing GenAI for Molecule Generation in Pharmaceuticals** Implementing a GenAI tool that allows researchers to input desired molecular properties and interactively generate potential drug candidates. The tool can provide real-time feedback on the viability

	of each generated molecule, helping scientists refine their search criteria and focus on the most promising compounds.
Quick Wins (Employee Tasks)	**Using GenAI to Draft Research Reports in Consumer Products** Deploying a GenAI tool where R&D staff can input raw experimental data and receive AI-generated drafts of research reports. Users can interactively edit and refine the content, ensuring the final reports meet publication standards and accurately represent the findings.
Changes (Single Department Processes)	**Deploying an AI Chatbot for Lab Management in Chemical Engineering** Implementing a GenAI-driven chatbot that lab personnel can interact with to manage inventory, schedule equipment usage, and troubleshoot experimental setups. The chatbot provides real-time assistance and can learn from user interactions to improve its recommendations and support.
Cross-Functional (Multi-Department Processes)	**Using GenAI to Streamline Product Development in Consumer Electronics** Utilizing a GenAI platform that integrates with design, engineering, and marketing departments to manage the product development lifecycle. Teams can input project requirements, and the AI generates design prototypes, suggests materials, and predicts market trends. The interactive

	platform allows for real-time collaboration and updates across departments, enhancing efficiency and innovation.
Transformational (New Business)	**Creating an AI-Driven Innovation Hub for Automotive R&D** Developing a new service that uses GenAI to drive innovation in automotive design and engineering. Researchers and designers can interact with the AI to generate and test new vehicle concepts, optimize aerodynamics, and simulate performance under various conditions. The platform provides real-time feedback and adapts to user inputs, accelerating the development of cutting-edge automotive technologies.

Importance of Synchronizing Technology, Governance, and Workforce in GenAI Initiatives

In many organizations, the IT department is often seen as the primary leader guiding the GenAI journey. While their expertise is crucial, relying solely on IT can create an imbalance. To truly unlock the potential of GenAI, it's essential that technology, governance, and workforce readiness advance in harmony. Misalignment among these three elements can lead to significant challenges as organizations progress through various AI initiatives.

When technology advances faster than governance and workforce readiness, confusion and inefficiency can arise. Imagine during the Proof of Concept stage, advanced GenAI tools are available, but without proper governance, there's no clear guidance on how to use these tools ethically and securely. This can lead to misuse or underuse of the technology, as employees are unsure of the boundaries and best practices. Moreover, without adequate workforce training, employees may struggle to leverage the technology fully, leading to missed opportunities for innovation and sub-optimal results.

In such scenarios, the organization might invest heavily in cutting-edge AI tools only to find that these tools are not being utilized effectively. Employees might lack the confidence to experiment with these technologies, fearing unintended consequences. This cautious approach can stifle innovation at a stage where creativity and experimentation are most needed. Additionally, the lack of governance can result in ethical breaches, such as biased decision-making or unauthorized data usage, which can have serious legal and reputational repercussions.

If governance frameworks lag behind technological advancements and workforce readiness, the organization risks encountering ethical and compliance issues. For example, during the Quick Wins phase, where GenAI solutions are implemented to improve specific tasks, a lack of robust governance can result in data privacy breaches or biased outputs. Employees might feel uncertain about the ethical implications of using GenAI, which can lead to resistance or misuse. Without clear policies and oversight, the organization may face legal and reputational risks, undermining the benefits of GenAI adoption.

In this stage, the organization might achieve some immediate gains from AI implementations, but these successes can be overshadowed by growing concerns about data security and ethical standards. Employees might misuse GenAI tools, either unintentionally or deliberately, due to the absence of clear guidelines. This misuse can lead to incidents that damage the organization's reputation and erode trust among stakeholders. Moreover, the lack of a governance framework can make it difficult to scale these quick wins into broader, more impactful initiatives.

When workforce readiness does not keep pace with technological and governance developments, the organization can experience inefficiencies and resistance to change. During the Changes (Single Department Processes) phase, employees may not be equipped with the necessary skills to utilize department-specific AI solutions effectively. This can lead to fragmented implementations and missed opportunities for cross-departmental learning and collaboration. Without a shared understanding of GenAI's potential, departments might develop isolated solutions that fail to integrate with the broader organizational context, leading to duplication of efforts and incompatible systems.

At this stage, the workforce's lack of readiness can manifest in several ways. Employees might resist adopting new AI tools, preferring to stick with familiar processes. This resistance can slow down the implementation of AI solutions and reduce their effectiveness. Additionally, without proper training, employees might misuse the tools, leading to inefficiencies and errors. The lack of cross-departmental collaboration can result in isolated pockets of AI adoption, where different departments develop their own solutions without considering the broader organizational needs. This siloed approach can lead to duplicated efforts, wasted resources, and incompatible systems that hinder the organization's overall progress.

To ensure a successful GenAI adoption, organizations must prioritize the synchronization of technology, governance, and workforce readiness. This involves:

- investing in the latest GenAI tools and ensuring they are accessible and user-friendly for all employees;
- continuously updating the technology stack to keep up with advancements;

- establishing clear and robust governance frameworks that include ethical guidelines, data management policies, and compliance with emerging regulations.

Regular reviews and updates to these policies are essential to keep pace with technological changes. The Implementation of comprehensive training programs that not only cover the technical aspects of GenAI, but also address the shifts in culture and mindset is key. Encouraging continuous learning and adaptability amongst employees is crucial.

By keeping technology, governance, and workforce readiness in sync, organizations can maximize the benefits of GenAI. At the Proof of Concept stage, with aligned technology, governance, and workforce readiness, organizations can foster a culture of innovation where employees understand the capabilities and limitations of GenAI, leading to realistic expectations and effective exploration of use cases. During the Quick Wins phase, proper alignment ensures that GenAI solutions are implemented efficiently, with employees fully equipped to leverage these tools. Clear governance policies mitigate risks, while a trained workforce maximizes productivity gains.

As initiatives progress to Changes, cross-departmental collaboration is enhanced when all three categories are aligned. This fosters the development of integrated solutions that contribute to the overall strategic goals of the organization. In the Cross-Functional (Multi-Department Processes) phase, alignment prevents fragmented processes and workarounds, ensuring a cohesive strategy for leveraging AI across the organization. This unified approach enhances productivity and strategic alignment. During the Transformational (New Business) phase, a synchronized approach enables organizations to innovate and scale new AI-driven business models effectively. Employees are empowered to drive these new models, resulting in successful initiatives and a competitive edge.

Aligning technology, governance, and workforce readiness requires a multifaceted approach. First, organizations must ensure that their technology investments are guided by clear strategic objectives. This means selecting GenAI tools that not only meet current needs but also have the flexibility to evolve with the organization's growth. Regularly updating the technology stack is essential to keep up with the rapid pace of AI advancements. Organizations should also foster an environment where employees feel comfortable experimenting with new tools, thereby promoting a culture of innovation and continuous improvement.

Simultaneously, robust governance frameworks must be established to guide the ethical and responsible use of GenAI. These frameworks should include clear guidelines on data management, ethical considerations, and compliance with regulations. Regular audits and reviews should be conducted to ensure that these policies remain relevant and effective. Governance frameworks should also be designed to promote transparency and accountability, thereby building trust among stakeholders.

Workforce readiness is another critical component. Organizations should invest in comprehensive training programs that equip employees with the necessary skills to use GenAI tools effectively. These programs should cover not only the technical aspects of GenAI but also the cultural and mindset shifts required to embrace these technologies. Encouraging continuous learning and adaptability among employees is crucial. Organizations should also create opportunities for cross-departmental collaboration, allowing employees to share insights and learn from each other's experiences.

As organizations embark on their GenAI journey, it is crucial to recognize that the success of these initiatives hinges on the alignment of technology, governance, and workforce readiness. By ensuring that these three elements advance in harmony, organizations can unlock the full potential of GenAI, driving innovation, efficiency, and competitive advantage in the ever-evolving business landscape.

In conclusion, the synchronization of technology, governance, and workforce readiness is not just a best practice; it is a necessity for organizations seeking to harness the power of GenAI. As we move forward, it is imperative that all departments work together, share knowledge, and remain committed to continuous improvement. By doing so, organizations can create a cohesive and dynamic environment where GenAI can thrive, leading to groundbreaking advancements and a sustainable competitive edge.

What's Next?

Looking ahead, the next chapter will delve into the critical role of governance in ensuring the responsible and ethical deployment of GenAI technologies. As organizations began to extensively experiment with generative AI models in 2024, issues like biased outputs, ethical dilemmas, and data privacy concerns surfaced, highlighting the need for robust governance frameworks. Part II: Governance Readiness—The Foundational Needs for AI Success will explore the key components of effective AI governance, including ethical guidelines, data management policies, compliance with emerging regulations, and the adoption of international standards and frameworks. By establishing a strong governance foundation, organizations can navigate the complexities of GenAI, mitigate risks, and ensure the sustainable and responsible integration of these technologies into their operations.

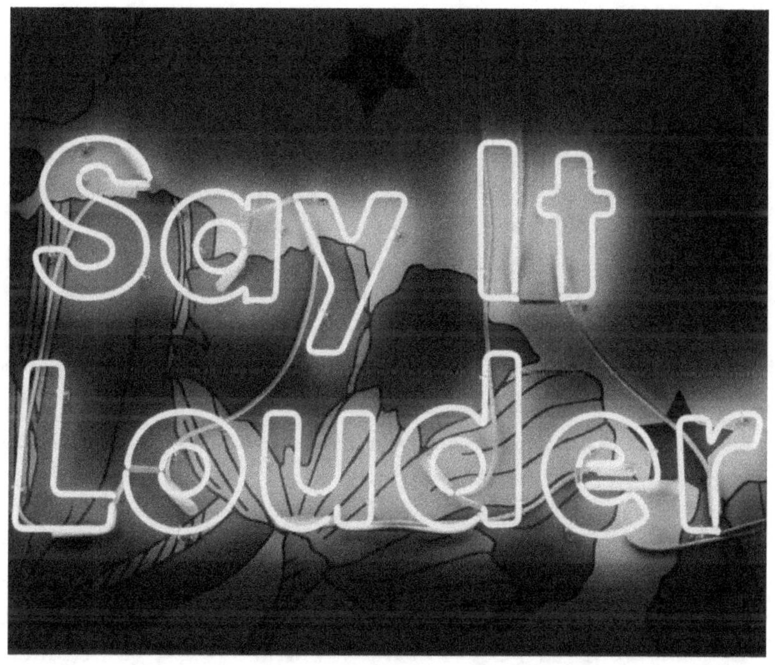
Say It
Louder

Part II:

Governance Readiness—The Foundational Needs for AI Success

In 2023, organizations across various industries began to extensively experiment with generative AI models, such as those used in text and image generation, natural language processing, and predictive analytics. These powerful tools demonstrated remarkable capabilities in creating content, analyzing data, and making predictions, offering the potential to revolutionize business processes and drive innovation. This surge in interest was accompanied by significant investments in AI technologies, with companies allocating substantial budgets to acquire advanced AI solutions and integrate them into their operations. The initial capital outlay and increased costs from vendors were seen as necessary steps to gain a competitive edge.

However, the investment in generative AI also highlighted the potential for a strong return on investment (ROI). Organizations anticipated that the efficiencies gained from automating routine tasks and enhancing decision-making would outweigh the initial expenses. Yet, this experimentation also underscored the pitfalls and challenges associated with these technologies, emphasizing the critical need for robust governance frameworks to ensure their responsible and ethical use.

As generative AI systems were deployed in real-world scenarios, organizations encountered a range of issues that underscored the importance of establishing clear guidelines and principles. One of the most pressing concerns was the potential for biased outputs, which could perpetuate or even amplify existing societal biases. For instance, AI-generated content, such as articles or social media posts, might reflect the biases present in the training data, leading to the dissemination of discriminatory or prejudiced information. Similarly, AI-powered recruitment tools could inadvertently favor certain demographics over others, raising questions about fairness and equal opportunity. Organizations quickly realized that without proactive measures to address these biases, the use of generative AI could lead to harmful consequences and damage their reputation.

Another significant challenge that emerged during the deployment of generative AI was the ethical dilemmas surrounding the use of large datasets for training these models. Many generative AI systems rely on vast amounts of data, often scraped from the internet or collected from various sources, to learn patterns and generate new content. However, this raised serious concerns about data privacy and security. In some cases, the data used for training might include sensitive personal information, such as medical records or financial details, which could be exposed or misused if not properly protected. Moreover, the collection and use of data without explicit consent or transparency could violate individuals' privacy rights and erode public trust in these technologies. Incidents of data misuse or breaches served as stark reminders of the importance of adhering to strict data governance policies and implementing robust security measures to safeguard personal information.

As the adoption of generative AI grew, organizations also had to navigate an evolving regulatory landscape. Governments and regulatory bodies around the world began to recognize the potential risks and challenges associated with AI technologies and started developing new regulations and guidelines to ensure their responsible use. Organizations closely monitored these emerging AI regulations and proactively adapted their policies and practices to remain compliant. This involved conducting thorough assessments of their AI systems, implementing transparency and accountability measures, and establishing clear processes for handling data and mitigating potential risks. Failure to comply with these regulations could result in significant legal and financial consequences, as well as reputational damage.

In addition to regulatory compliance, organizations also looked towards international standards and frameworks for guidance on AI governance. They recognized that AI governance was not just a local or national issue, but a global one that required collaboration and alignment across borders. International organizations, such as the IEEE and ISO, developed standards and best practices for the ethical development and deployment of AI systems. These frameworks provided valuable guidance on topics such as transparency, accountability, fairness, and privacy, helping organizations to establish a common language and approach to AI governance. By aligning with these international standards, organizations could demonstrate their commitment to responsible AI practices and build trust with their stakeholders.

The dynamic and rapidly evolving nature of AI technologies, especially generative AI, presented ongoing challenges for organizations. As these technologies advanced and new applications emerged, organizations had to continuously monitor and assess the risks and potential impacts associated with their use. This required the establishment of robust risk assessment processes that could identify and mitigate potential issues before they escalated. Regular audits, impact assessments, and stakeholder engagement were essential to ensure that AI systems remained aligned with organizational values and societal expectations. Organizations also had to be prepared to adapt and update their governance frameworks as new risks and challenges emerged, ensuring that they remained effective and relevant in the face of technological change.

The experiences and lessons learned from the deployment of generative AI in 2023 led to a significant cultural shift within organizations. There was a growing recognition that responsible AI governance was not just a compliance requirement, but a fundamental aspect of organizational ethics and values. Leaders began to understand that the success and long-term sustainability of AI initiatives depended on building trust with stakeholders, including employees, customers, and the wider public. This required a proactive and transparent approach to AI governance, where the potential risks and benefits of these technologies were openly discussed and addressed.

Organizations started to integrate AI governance into their overall organizational ethos, making it a core part of their business strategy and decision-making processes. This involved establishing dedicated AI governance teams, providing training and education to employees, and fostering a culture of responsible innovation. By embedding AI governance into the fabric of the organization, companies could ensure that ethical considerations were not an afterthought, but an integral part of every AI project and initiative.

The cultural shift towards responsible AI also extended beyond individual organizations, leading to increased collaboration and knowledge-sharing across industries and sectors. Companies recognized that the challenges and opportunities presented by generative AI were not unique to their own operations but were shared by others in their ecosystem. This led to the formation of industry-wide consortia and working groups, where organizations could come together to develop common standards, share best practices, and address collective challenges. By working together, organizations could leverage their collective expertise and resources to drive responsible AI innovation and ensure that the benefits of these technologies were realized while minimizing the risks.

The extensive experimentation with generative AI models in 2023 served as a wake-up call for organizations, highlighting the urgent need for robust governance frameworks to ensure the responsible and ethical use of these powerful technologies. The challenges and risks associated with biased outputs, data privacy, and regulatory compliance underscored the importance of proactive measures and clear guidelines to mitigate potential harms. By closely monitoring emerging regulations, aligning with international standards, and establishing continuous risk assessment processes, organizations could navigate the complex landscape of AI governance and build trust with their stakeholders. The cultural shift towards responsible AI, driven by the integration of governance into the organizational ethos and increased collaboration across industries, marked a significant step forward in the journey towards realizing the full potential of generative AI while safeguarding the interests of individuals and society as a whole.

Importance of Governance Readiness in AI Integration

Governance Readiness is key to successfully bringing AI into a company's workflow. It's about fully grasping the tech, involving key players, handling risks, and setting clear rules and support. This thorough method makes sure AI efforts match the company's aims, meet legal and ethical norms, and benefit everyone involved.

Let's take a broader look into its importance.

Alignment With Organization Goals

Governance readiness plays a vital role in ensuring that AI initiatives are aligned with the broader goals and strategies of the organization. This alignment is crucial for achieving desired outcomes and maximizing the value of AI investments. When AI projects are not properly aligned with organizational objectives, they risk becoming isolated efforts that fail to deliver meaningful results or, worse, may even work against the company's overall mission.

One of the primary ways governance readiness facilitates alignment is by establishing a clear and comprehensive AI strategy. This strategy should be developed in close collaboration with key stakeholders across the organization, including executive leadership, business unit heads, and IT professionals. By engaging these stakeholders in the planning process, organizations can ensure that AI initiatives are prioritized based on their potential to contribute to the company's strategic goals.

A well-defined AI strategy should outline the organization's vision for how AI will be used to drive business value, as well as the specific objectives and key performance indicators that will be used to measure success. This strategy should also take into account the organization's existing capabilities, resources, and constraints, as well as the competitive landscape and industry trends. By grounding AI initiatives in a clear strategic framework, governance readiness helps to ensure that these efforts are focused, purposeful, and aligned with the bigger picture.

Governance readiness also supports alignment by establishing a structured process for evaluating and prioritizing AI projects. This process should involve a rigorous assessment of each project's potential benefits, risks, and resource requirements, as well as its alignment with the organization's overall AI strategy. By subjecting AI initiatives to a consistent and transparent evaluation process, organizations can ensure that they are allocating their resources to the projects that are most likely to deliver strategic value.

Governance readiness promotes alignment by establishing clear lines of communication and accountability for AI initiatives. When roles and responsibilities for AI projects are clearly defined and communicated, it becomes easier to ensure that everyone is working towards the same goals and that progress is being tracked and reported in a consistent manner. Governance readiness also helps to ensure that AI initiatives are subject to regular review and adjustment based on changing business needs and priorities. By establishing a framework for ongoing monitoring and course correction, organizations can ensure that their AI efforts remain aligned with their overall strategy even as circumstances change.

Facilitation of Compliance and Ethical Standards

Governance readiness is crucial for facilitating compliance with legal and regulatory requirements, as well as upholding ethical standards in AI projects. As AI technologies become more prevalent and sophisticated, organizations must navigate an increasingly complex landscape of laws, regulations, and societal expectations. Failure to comply with these requirements can result in significant legal liabilities, reputational damage, and erosion of public trust.

A robust governance framework helps organizations proactively identify and address potential compliance and ethical risks associated with AI deployment. This includes ensuring adherence to data privacy regulations. Governance readiness also involves establishing clear policies and procedures for managing issues such as algorithmic bias, transparency, and accountability in AI decision-making.

By incorporating legal and ethical considerations into every stage of the AI lifecycle, from project planning and design to deployment and monitoring, organizations can mitigate the risk of non-compliance and unintended consequences. This requires close collaboration between AI teams, legal experts, and ethics committees to ensure that AI initiatives are developed and implemented in a responsible and compliant manner.

Governance readiness also plays a vital role in maintaining trust with stakeholders, including customers, employees, and the wider public. By demonstrating a commitment to legal and ethical standards, organizations can build confidence in their AI initiatives and foster a culture of responsible innovation. This trust is essential for driving adoption, attracting talent, and securing the social license to operate in an increasingly AI-driven world.

As AI regulations continue to evolve and vary across jurisdictions, governance readiness helps organizations stay agile and adapt to changing requirements. By establishing a flexible and proactive governance framework, organizations can quickly respond to new laws and regulations, as well as emerging ethical concerns and societal expectations.

Risk Mitigation

Proper governance is essential for identifying and mitigating the various risks associated with AI projects. As organizations increasingly rely on AI technologies to drive business value, they must be prepared to manage a wide range of potential risks, including data breaches, biased decision-making, and operational disruptions. Failure to effectively mitigate these risks can result in significant financial losses, legal liabilities, and reputational damage.

Another significant risk associated with AI projects is biased decision-making. AI algorithms can inadvertently perpetuate or amplify existing biases in the data they are trained on, leading to discriminatory outcomes. For example, an AI system used for hiring decisions may be biased against certain demographic groups if the training data reflects historical hiring patterns. Governance readiness helps organizations mitigate this risk by establishing clear guidelines for data selection and model training, as well as implementing regular audits and testing to detect and correct biases.

Operational disruptions are another key risk associated with AI projects. As organizations increasingly rely on AI systems to automate critical business processes, any disruptions or failures can have significant impacts on operations and customer service. Governance readiness helps organizations mitigate this risk by establishing clear policies and procedures for AI system development, testing, and deployment. This includes implementing robust monitoring and alerting systems to quickly detect and respond to any issues, as well as establishing clear contingency plans and backup systems to ensure business continuity.

Effective AI governance also involves ongoing risk assessment and management. As AI technologies and business environments evolve, new risks may emerge, and existing risks may change in nature or severity. Governance readiness helps organizations stay ahead of these changes by establishing regular risk assessment processes and adapting governance frameworks as needed. This includes conducting periodic audits and impact assessments to identify and prioritize risks, as well as engaging with stakeholders to gather feedback and insights.

Governance readiness helps organizations build a culture of risk awareness and accountability around AI projects. By establishing clear roles and responsibilities for risk management, as well as providing training and resources to support risk mitigation efforts, organizations can ensure that everyone involved in AI projects is working towards the same goal of responsible and secure AI deployment.

Promoting Stakeholder Confidence

Effective governance structures play a crucial role in promoting stakeholder confidence in the AI implementation process. When stakeholders, including employees, management, and customers, perceive that an organization has a robust governance framework in place, they are more likely to trust and support AI initiatives. This confidence is essential for driving adoption, fostering collaboration, and realizing the full potential of AI technologies.

One of the primary ways governance promotes stakeholder confidence is by establishing transparency and accountability in the AI implementation process. When stakeholders understand how AI systems are being developed, deployed, and monitored, they are more likely to trust that these systems are being used in a responsible and ethical manner. Governance frameworks should include clear communication channels and reporting mechanisms to keep stakeholders informed about AI projects and their potential impacts.

Governance structures also promote stakeholder confidence by ensuring that AI initiatives are aligned with the organization's values and ethical principles. Stakeholders are more likely to support AI projects when they believe that these projects are being undertaken in a way that is consistent with the organization's mission and values. By establishing clear ethical guidelines and oversight mechanisms, governance frameworks help to ensure that AI initiatives are not only technically sound but also morally and socially responsible.

Another way governance fosters stakeholder confidence is by providing opportunities for stakeholder engagement and input. When stakeholders feel that their concerns and perspectives are being heard and taken into account, they are more likely to support AI initiatives. Governance frameworks should include mechanisms for soliciting and incorporating stakeholder feedback, such as surveys, focus groups, and advisory committees. By actively engaging stakeholders in the governance process, organizations can build trust and ensure that AI initiatives are responsive to the needs and concerns of all relevant parties.

In addition, governance structures enhance stakeholder confidence by ensuring that AI initiatives are subject to regular review and evaluation. When stakeholders know that AI systems are being continuously monitored and assessed for performance, fairness, and safety, they are more likely to trust that these systems are being used in a responsible and effective manner. Governance frameworks should include processes for regular auditing, testing, and reporting on AI systems, as well as mechanisms for addressing any issues or concerns that arise.

Furthermore, governance demonstrates an organization's commitment to responsible AI innovation. When stakeholders see that an organization is investing in governance structures and processes, they are more likely to believe that the organization is taking AI seriously and is committed to using these technologies in a way that benefits all stakeholders. This commitment can help to build trust and support for AI initiatives, both within the organization and among external stakeholders such as customers, partners, and regulators.

Enabling Scalability and Sustainability

Governance readiness is crucial for enabling the scalability and sustainability of AI solutions within an organization. As AI initiatives move beyond initial pilots and proofs of concept, it is essential to have a robust governance framework in place to ensure that these solutions can be effectively scaled and maintained over time.

Governance readiness also enables scalability by ensuring that AI solutions are designed with long-term sustainability in mind. This includes considering factors such as data quality, model performance, and infrastructure requirements, as well as planning for ongoing maintenance and updates. By taking a proactive approach to these issues, organizations can avoid the pitfalls of AI solutions that quickly become outdated or unreliable, and instead build solutions that continue to deliver value over time.

In addition to enabling scalability, governance readiness is essential for ensuring the long-term sustainability of AI solutions. This includes establishing processes for monitoring and evaluating the performance of AI systems over time, as well as mechanisms for addressing any issues or concerns that arise. Governance frameworks should also include provisions for ongoing training and education to ensure that AI teams have the skills and knowledge needed to maintain and update AI solutions as technologies and business needs evolve.

Supporting Continuous Improvement

Governance readiness provides a critical framework for supporting continuous improvement in AI systems. By establishing processes for monitoring performance, gathering feedback, and making necessary adjustments, governance frameworks enable organizations to continuously refine and optimize their AI solutions over time.

This includes setting up mechanisms for tracking key performance indicators and metrics, such as accuracy, efficiency, and user satisfaction, as well as establishing channels for collecting feedback from stakeholders, including employees, customers, and partners.

Governance frameworks also provide a structured approach for evaluating this data and feedback, identifying areas for improvement, and implementing changes and updates to AI systems as needed. By institutionalizing these processes for continuous improvement, governance readiness helps organizations to stay agile and responsive in the face of evolving technologies, business needs, and stakeholder expectations, ensuring that AI initiatives continue to deliver value and drive positive outcomes over the long term.

Essential Components of Organizational Readiness for Leaders

From the perspective of organizational readiness, the following components, shown below, are crucial for leaders as they provide the "guard rails" needed to successfully manage change within an organization.

CATEGORY	COMPONENT	Proof of Concept (Experiments)	Quick Wins (Employee Tasks)	Changes (Single Department Processes)	Cross Functional (Multi-Department Processes)	Transformational (New Business)
GOVERNANCE	Steering Leadership	●	●	●	●	●
	Ethics & Responsible Use	●	●	●	●	●
	Legal	●	●	●	●	●
	Usage		●	●	●	●

CHANGE COMPLEXITY & RISK →

Steering Leadership

Steering Leadership plays a crucial role in guiding AI initiatives within an organization. Effective steering leadership ensures that AI projects align with the organization's strategic goals and values, and that they are implemented in a way that maximizes their potential benefits while minimizing risks.

As companies undertake more complex AI initiatives, the role of leadership evolves from simply sanctioning projects to actively understanding AI capabilities and limitations, setting clear objectives, and ensuring that AI aligns with broader business strategies. This requires leaders to have a deep understanding of the technology, its potential applications, and the challenges and opportunities it presents.

However, effective steering leadership in AI initiatives is not just about top-down directives. It requires an inclusive approach that involves multiple key areas of the organization. As AI projects grow in complexity, the integration of diverse perspectives becomes essential to ensure that they are successful and sustainable.

Some of the key areas that should be involved in steering leadership for AI initiatives are included below.

Human Resources

HR plays a crucial role in managing the workforce implications of AI adoption. As AI technologies advance, HR must assess changing skill requirements, develop strategies to acquire and develop necessary competencies, and manage potential workforce restructuring. This involves conducting skill gap analyses, developing training and upskilling programs, and supporting employees affected by job role changes or displacement. Additionally, HR is responsible for fostering a culture receptive to

AI-driven change by communicating benefits and implications, addressing concerns, and promoting continuous learning. By proactively managing these aspects, HR ensures the organization has the talent and mindset to successfully leverage AI technologies.

Legal Department

The Legal Department plays a crucial role in navigating the complex legal landscape of AI. They work closely with AI development teams to implement appropriate data governance policies, consent mechanisms, and anonymization techniques to mitigate legal risks. Their expertise is essential in addressing the dangers of copyright infringement, which can arise from the unauthorized use of copyrighted material in the training and deployment of AI systems.

Moreover, the Legal Department is responsible for addressing the intellectual property implications of AI, such as securing patents and copyrights for newly developed algorithms and models. They must also ensure that the organization has the necessary licenses and permissions to use third-party AI technologies. Additionally, the Legal Department must stay informed about evolving AI-specific regulations related to algorithmic transparency, bias, and accountability. By proactively engaging with these legal issues, the Legal Department helps to ensure that the organization's AI initiatives are legally compliant, ethically sound, and socially responsible, thereby mitigating potential legal risks associated with AI deployment.

Finance

The Finance team plays a critical role in steering AI initiatives by providing financial oversight and guidance. They are responsible for budgeting, forecasting, and ensuring that AI investments align with the organization's overall financial goals. This involves carefully evaluating the potential costs and benefits of AI projects, including the required infrastructure, talent, and ongoing maintenance expenses.

The Finance team works closely with other departments to develop detailed financial projections for AI initiatives, taking into account factors such as scalability, return on investment, and potential risks. They provide valuable insights into the financial implications of AI projects, helping decision-makers understand the long-term impact on the organization's bottom line. By carefully monitoring and analyzing the financial performance of AI investments, the Finance team helps to ensure that the organization is allocating its resources effectively and efficiently, balancing the need for innovation with fiscal responsibility.

Information Technology

Information Technology (IT) plays a vital role in the successful implementation and integration of AI solutions within an organization. Their expertise is essential in ensuring that AI initiatives are supported by a robust and secure IT infrastructure, capable of handling the vast amounts of data and computational power required by these technologies.

The IT department works closely with AI development teams to design and implement the necessary hardware and software systems, including servers, storage solutions, and networking components. They also ensure that these systems are scalable, allowing for the growth and expansion of AI initiatives over time. Additionally, IT is responsible for implementing appropriate security measures to protect sensitive data and prevent unauthorized access, which is crucial given the large volumes of data often involved in AI projects.

Another key aspect of IT's role is ensuring that AI technologies are compatible with existing systems and processes. This involves carefully evaluating the organization's current IT landscape and identifying any potential integration challenges. IT works to develop solutions that allow for seamless integration of AI technologies with existing software and hardware, minimizing disruption to business operations. By leveraging their technical expertise and understanding of the organization's IT ecosystem, the IT department plays a critical role in ensuring the successful deployment and long-term viability of AI initiatives.

Operations

The Operations team plays a crucial role in the successful implementation of AI initiatives by providing valuable insights into how these technologies can optimize business processes. Their deep understanding of the organization's day-to-day operations and workflows is essential for identifying areas where AI can deliver the most significant impact.

The Operations team works closely with AI development teams to map out existing processes and identify potential inefficiencies or bottlenecks. They provide practical insights into how tasks are currently performed, what challenges are faced, and where there are opportunities for improvement. This collaboration helps guide the development of AI solutions that are tailored to the specific needs of the organization, ensuring that they deliver measurable enhancements to operational efficiency and effectiveness.

By leveraging the practical insights and expertise of the Operations team, organizations can develop AI initiatives that drive tangible improvements in productivity, quality, and overall operational performance.

Marketing and Sales

The Marketing and Sales departments play a vital role in the development of AI initiatives by providing valuable insights into customer behaviors and market trends. Their deep understanding of customer needs, preferences, and pain points is essential for creating AI solutions that deliver tangible value to the organization's target audience.

Marketing and Sales teams can offer unique perspectives on how AI technologies can be leveraged to enhance the customer experience, improve engagement, and drive business growth. For example, they can provide insights into how AI-powered personalization can be used to deliver more relevant and targeted marketing messages, or how AI-driven chatbots can be deployed to improve customer support and service.

Moreover, Marketing and Sales can help identify emerging market trends and opportunities that can be addressed through AI initiatives. By staying attuned to the evolving needs and expectations of customers, these teams can guide the development of AI solutions that are not only technically advanced but also aligned with the organization's strategic goals and market positioning.

The collaboration between Marketing, Sales, and AI development teams is crucial for creating solutions that are not only innovative but also commercially viable. By leveraging the insights and expertise of these departments, organizations can ensure that their AI initiatives are customer-centric, delivering real value to their target audience and driving measurable business growth.

The participation of these diverse departments ensures a holistic approach to AI initiatives. It allows for the consideration of various perspectives, from ethical and legal concerns to technical feasibility and financial viability. This collaborative approach not only enhances the effectiveness of AI strategies but also fosters an organizational culture that is more receptive to embracing AI-driven change.

Important Considerations for Leaders

There are crucial considerations for leaders when guiding their organizations through the complex landscape of AI adoption. One of the key considerations is the formation and utilization of Steering Committees.

- **Formation and Utilization of Steering Committees:** Steering Committees typically form early in an organization's AI journey, either before, during, or after the launch of several Proof of Concepts. They serve as a crucial component in setting the priorities and defining the role of Generative AI within the organization.

- **Recognition of Steering Committees' Value:** Leaders should recognize the value of Steering Committees and actively leverage this forum to seek guidance, approvals, and sponsorship in addressing potential challenges. The Steering Committee provides a platform for leaders to engage with key stakeholders, including senior leadership, subject matter experts, and representatives from various departments. By presenting their AI initiatives to the committee, leaders can gain valuable insights, align their efforts with organizational priorities, and secure the necessary support and resources to drive successful implementation.

- **Proactive Approach in the Absence of Holistic Leadership:** In situations where holistic steering leadership is absent, leaders must be proactive in addressing this gap. They should approach their sponsors and advocate for the implementation of the necessary leadership partnerships. This may involve identifying key individuals who can champion the AI initiatives, building alliances across different departments, and establishing a shared vision for the role of GenAI within the organization. By taking a proactive approach and fostering collaborative partnerships, leaders can lay the foundation for successful AI adoption, even in the absence of a formal Steering Committee.

- **Effective Leadership and Cross-Functional Collaboration:** Ultimately, the success of AI initiatives relies heavily on effective leadership and cross-functional collaboration. Leaders must navigate the complexities of their organization's AI journey with strategic foresight, adaptability, and a commitment to driving meaningful change. By leveraging Steering Committees, building strong partnerships, and proactively addressing challenges, leaders can position their organizations for success in the era of GenAI.

Ethics and Responsible Use

As organizations embrace Generative AI, they must navigate the ethical implications and ensure responsible use of these technologies. GenAI introduces concerns regarding data privacy, algorithmic bias, transparency, and accountability. To keep pace with evolving societal and regulatory expectations, companies must establish ethical guidelines and develop comprehensive frameworks as AI use becomes more sophisticated. This involves addressing issues such as data protection, fairness, explainability, and ongoing monitoring to ensure AI systems align with organizational values and societal norms. By prioritizing ethics and responsible use, organizations can build trust, mitigate risks, and harness the benefits of AI while upholding the highest standards of integrity.

Consider the ethical guidelines that organizations are typically expected to adhere to.

Establishing Core Principles for Ethical AI

To ensure responsible AI use, organizations must define clear ethical guidelines focusing on fairness, transparency, accountability, and privacy. Aligning with international standards and regulations, such as the EU AI Act, is crucial for maintaining compliance and building trust. By establishing these core principles as the foundation of their AI initiatives, organizations can navigate the ethical landscape with confidence and integrity.

Developing Policies for Ethical AI Management

Organizations must develop a comprehensive code of conduct for AI development and usage, outlining clear guidelines and best practices. Additionally, implementing a risk assessment framework is crucial for identifying and mitigating potential ethical risks associated with AI projects. By establishing robust policies and management practices, organizations can ensure that their AI initiatives align with ethical principles and minimize unintended consequences.

Promoting AI Ethics Through Education and Training

To foster a culture of ethical AI, organizations should launch company-wide awareness programs that educate employees about the importance of AI ethics and its implications for their work. Furthermore, targeted training should be provided to teams directly involved in AI development and deployment, focusing on ethical design principles and best practices. By investing in education and training initiatives, organizations can ensure that their workforce is equipped with the knowledge and skills necessary to develop and use AI responsibly.

Embedding Ethics Into AI Business Processes

To ensure that ethical considerations are integral to AI initiatives, organizations should adopt an "Ethics by Design" approach, incorporating ethical principles into every stage of the AI development lifecycle. This involves establishing clear processes for ethical review and approval of AI projects, ensuring that potential risks and concerns are addressed proactively. By embedding ethics into core business processes, organizations can maintain the highest standards of responsible AI development and deployment.

Fostering Communication and Transparency in AI Ethics

Organizations should prioritize regular internal communication to reinforce the importance of AI ethics among all employees. This involves sharing updates, best practices, and lessons learned to maintain a strong ethical culture. Additionally, maintaining transparency with external stakeholders about the organization's AI ethics practices is crucial for building trust and accountability. By openly communicating their commitment to responsible AI development and deployment, organizations can foster a positive reputation and strengthen relationships with customers, partners, and the broader community.

Ensuring Ethical Compliance Through Monitoring and Auditing

To maintain the highest standards of ethical AI, organizations must establish systems for continuous monitoring of AI applications. This involves tracking key metrics, identifying potential issues, and taking corrective action when necessary. Regular audits should also be conducted to assess adherence to ethical standards and identify areas for improvement. By implementing robust monitoring and auditing processes, organizations can proactively identify and address ethical risks, ensuring that their AI systems remain compliant and trustworthy over time.

Encouraging Feedback and Continuous Improvement in AI Ethics

Organizations should create accessible channels for employees to report concerns or provide feedback on AI ethics. This feedback mechanism is essential for identifying potential issues, gathering insights, and fostering a culture of open communication. Additionally, organizations must commit to continuous improvement by regularly reviewing and updating their AI ethics policies and practices based on employee feedback, evolving industry standards, and emerging best practices. By actively seeking feedback and embracing a mindset of ongoing improvement, organizations can ensure that their AI ethics framework remains relevant, effective, and responsive to the changing landscape of AI technology.

Important Considerations for Leaders

There are several critical steps that leaders need to take to effectively implement an AI Ethics and Responsible Use policy. These steps ensure the ethical deployment of AI technologies and mitigate potential risks.

- **Educate and Engage:** Educate leadership and stakeholders about the importance of an AI Ethics and Responsible Use policy. Highlight the potential risks, legal implications, and ethical considerations associated with AI use. Provide examples of challenges faced by organizations lacking such policies.

- **Assess and Raise Awareness:** Assess the current state of AI usage in the organization. Identify potential ethical risks and areas lacking oversight. Raise awareness among stakeholders about the importance of ethical AI use and the risks of not having a policy.

- **Benchmark and Research:** Investigate industry best practices and standards regarding AI ethics. Research how similar organizations have implemented their AI ethics policies. Use this information to guide the development of your organization's policy.

- **Engage Stakeholders:** Engage with a diverse group of stakeholders, including AI developers, users, ethical experts, legal advisors, and leadership. Gather input to understand various perspectives and concerns related to AI usage in the organization.

- **Draft the Policy:** Based on research and stakeholder input, draft a comprehensive AI Ethics and Responsible

Use policy. Include guidelines on data privacy, fairness, transparency, accountability, and safety. Ensure alignment with the organization's values and legal requirements.

- **Review and Approve:** Present the draft policy to the leadership team for review and approval. Iterate on the policy based on feedback received.

- **Implement and Train:** Once approved, implement the policy across the organization. Train employees on the new guidelines and integrate the policy into existing workflows. Ensure compliance of all AI systems and projects with the policy.

- **Monitor and Evaluate:** Establish mechanisms to monitor compliance with the policy and evaluate its effectiveness. Conduct regular audits, gather feedback, and update the policy as needed based on technological advancements or changes in ethical standards.

- **Communicate:** Communicate the policy and its importance to the entire organization. Ensure that everyone understands the ethical considerations in AI usage and their role in upholding these standards.

- **Continuously Improve:** Treat the policy as a living document that evolves with emerging AI technologies and ethical considerations. Assign ownership of the policy to the appropriate function and ensure ongoing updates and improvements.

Legal

The legal component encompasses compliance with laws and regulations related to AI. Early in AI adoption, this might focus on data privacy laws and intellectual property rights. As organizations scale their AI efforts, legal considerations become more complex, including international regulations, sector-specific AI governance, and emerging laws specifically targeting AI technologies. Companies need to continuously update their legal strategies to manage risks effectively.

These can include the following considerations:

- **Scope and Application:** What aspects of AI the policy covers, such as AI development, procurement, usage, and data management. Clearly defining the scope ensures that all relevant activities are subject to legal scrutiny and compliance procedures.

- **Compliance With Laws and Regulations:** Include adherence to international, national, and local laws related to AI, such as data privacy (GDPR, CCPA), nondiscrimination, and intellectual property rights. Legal compliance is fundamental in avoiding penalties and maintaining operational legitimacy. For example, companies operating in Europe must comply with the General Data Protection Regulation (GDPR), which has stringent requirements for data protection and privacy.

- **Data Governance:** Outline rules for data acquisition, storage, processing, and sharing, ensuring compliance with data protection regulations. Effective data governance policies ensure that data is managed ethically and lawfully, minimizing risks of data breaches and ensuring that AI models are built on reliable data sources.

- **AI Transparency and Explainability:** Mandate the use of transparent AI systems where decisions can be explained in understandable terms, particularly for critical applications. Transparency in AI fosters trust among stakeholders and ensures that AI-driven decisions can be audited and understood, which is crucial for applications in healthcare, finance, and legal sectors.

- **Risk Management:** Include guidelines for identifying, assessing, and mitigating risks associated with AI, including technical, legal, and reputational risks. Comprehensive risk management strategies help in proactively addressing potential issues that could arise from AI deployment, such as bias in AI algorithms or unintended consequences in decision-making systems.

- **Intellectual Property:** Clarify the ownership and usage rights of AI-generated content and inventions. Protecting intellectual property is vital for maintaining competitive advantage and ensuring that innovations derived from AI are legally safeguarded. This includes understanding patent laws and copyright issues related to AI-generated works.

- **Training and Awareness:** Mandate regular training for employees on legal and ethical aspects of AI. Continual education ensures that employees are aware of the latest legal requirements and ethical considerations, promoting a culture of compliance and responsibility within the organization.

- **Audit and Compliance Monitoring:** Establish procedures for regular audits of AI systems to ensure compliance with legal, ethical, and company standards. Regular audits help in detecting and rectifying any deviations from established protocols, ensuring that AI systems remain within the bounds of legal and ethical guidelines.

- **Reporting and Accountability:** Create mechanisms for reporting AI-related issues and designate responsible personnel or departments. Establishing clear channels for reporting issues related to AI use helps in prompt resolution and accountability, ensuring that any legal or ethical concerns are addressed swiftly and effectively.

By integrating these considerations, companies can build a robust legal framework for AI that not only ensures compliance but also fosters innovation and trust among stakeholders.

Important Considerations for Leaders

GenAI is fallible and can also be manipulated. An organization must be prepared to address potential issues that can arise. Employees need to understand how to identify and report potential issues. Below are some examples:

- **Bias in AI Systems:** AI algorithms can inherit biases present in their training data. This can lead to unfair or discriminatory outcomes. For example, a recruitment AI might favor male candidates over female candidates if it was trained on historical data where males were predominantly hired.

- **Lack of Explainability:** Many AI models are often seen as "black boxes." They can provide outputs without clear explanations on how they arrived at those decisions. This can be problematic in critical applications like healthcare, where doctors need to understand the rationale behind a diagnosis suggested by an AI.

- **Data Privacy Concerns:** AI systems often require large amounts of data, which can include sensitive personal information. There's a risk that this data could be mishandled, leading to privacy breaches. An example is facial recognition technology, where the collection and storage of facial data raise significant privacy issues.

- **Security Vulnerabilities:** AI systems can be susceptible to various forms of attacks, such as data poisoning or adversarial attacks, where slight, often imperceptible, alterations to input data can lead to incorrect outputs. A notorious example is altering a stop sign in a way that causes an autonomous vehicle to misidentify it as a different sign, potentially leading to accidents.

- **AI Manipulation and Misuse:** There's a risk of AI being used for malicious purposes, such as deepfakes in creating misleading or false media. For example, deepfake technology can be used to create fake videos of public figures saying or doing things they never actually did, leading to misinformation.

Leaders should request and review any documentation related to the above with their sponsors and the organization's Legal team to ensure that any materials being distributed to employees are compliant with their efforts.

Usage

This refers to how AI is utilized within the organization and can be considered a summation of the readiness components already discussed.

Initially, AI usage might be limited to specific PoCs. As companies grow more adept, AI usage expands, integrating into various business processes and decision-making—increasing potential risks and liability exposure for organizations. This necessitates the need for a Use Policy. A typical Use Policy will include some or all of the following:

- **Purpose of the Policy:** This section outlines the primary goals and objectives of the AI Use Policy. It ensures that everyone within the organization understands the importance of having guidelines in place to manage AI technologies effectively. The purpose may include promoting ethical AI use, mitigating risks, and ensuring compliance with laws and regulations, thereby creating a safe and productive environment for AI integration.

- **Scope and Applicability:** This part defines who and what is covered by the AI Use Policy. It clarifies whether the policy applies to all employees, contractors, and third-party vendors and whether it covers all types of AI applications used within the organization. By clearly defining the scope, the organization ensures that all relevant stakeholders are aware of and adhere to the AI guidelines.

- **Commitment to Ethical AI Use With Guidelines for Ethical Decision-Making in AI Implementation:** This section underscores the organization's dedication to ethical AI practices. It provides guidelines for making ethical decisions in the development, deployment, and use of AI systems. Topics may include fairness, transparency, accountability, and the avoidance of bias, ensuring that AI implementations align with the organization's values and ethical standards.

- **Privacy and Compliance With Applicable Laws:** Here, the policy details the organization's commitment to protecting user privacy and adhering to relevant legal requirements. It outlines the steps and measures taken to ensure that AI systems comply with data protection laws, such as GDPR or CCPA, and emphasizes the importance of handling personal data responsibly and securely.

- **Ownership of AI-Generated Content:** This point clarifies who holds the rights to content created by AI systems. It addresses intellectual property concerns, specifying whether the organization or the individual who developed the AI holds ownership. This ensures that there is no ambiguity regarding the rights and usage of AI-generated materials.

- **Licensing Agreements and Copyright Considerations:** This section provides guidelines on managing licensing agreements and copyright issues related to AI technologies. It emphasizes the importance of complying with licensing terms for AI software and models and addresses the legal implications of using external intellectual property within AI systems.

- **Labeling Outputs Indicating That They Were Created by AI:** To promote transparency, this part of the policy mandates that AI-generated outputs be clearly labeled. This helps users distinguish between human-created and AI-generated content, fostering trust and ensuring that the use of AI is transparent to all stakeholders.

- **Guidelines for Using External Intellectual Property in AI Models:** This section offers best practices for incorporating external intellectual property into AI models. It emphasizes the importance of obtaining appropriate licenses and permissions and ensures that the use of such intellectual property complies with legal and ethical standards.

- **AI System Security Protocols:** This point outlines the security measures required to protect AI systems from threats and vulnerabilities. It includes protocols for safeguarding data, maintaining system integrity, and ensuring the resilience of AI technologies against cyber-attacks, thereby minimizing risks to the organization.

- **Incident Response and Reporting Mechanisms:** This section details the procedures for responding to and reporting incidents involving AI systems. It includes steps for identifying, assessing, and mitigating the impact of AI-related issues and establishes a clear process for escalating and reporting incidents to appropriate authorities within the organization.

- **Vendor Compliance With Company's Ethical Standards:** This part ensures that third-party vendors providing AI technologies comply with the organization's ethical standards. It requires vendors to adhere to the same guidelines and practices, ensuring consistency and integrity in the use of AI across the supply chain.

- **Regular Review and Update of AI Policies:** To keep up with the rapid advancements in AI technology, this section mandates the regular review and updating of the AI Use Policy. It ensures that the policy remains relevant and effective, reflecting new developments, regulatory changes, and emerging risks.

- **Metrics for Measuring AI Impact and Performance:** This point focuses on establishing metrics to evaluate the performance and impact of AI systems. It includes guidelines for measuring the effectiveness, efficiency, and outcomes of AI implementations, helping the organization to assess the value and risks associated with its AI initiatives.

By providing detailed explanations for each point, the AI Use Policy ensures comprehensive guidance for ethical, legal, and effective AI integration within the organization.

Important Considerations for Leaders

There are indicators that can help leaders determine if adoption risks may occur resulting from an organization's Technology Architecture Readiness for AI.

- **PoC Teams:** Ensure that PoC teams include individuals with knowledge of Ethical and Responsible Use, access to legal resources, and the support of Steering Leadership. Implement missing readiness components ASAP.

- **AI Maturity:** As the organization matures in working with GenAI and expands into more complex initiatives, develop a comprehensive Use Policy to ensure employees understand the ramifications, policies, and procedures for using the technology safely.

- **Organizational Readiness:** Make the Use Policy available as part of the change efforts supporting Quick Wins, where a larger number of employees with varying degrees of knowledge need to be aligned on the organization's Point of View.

By addressing these considerations, leaders can effectively guide their organizations through the adoption and implementation of AI initiatives while mitigating risks and ensuring responsible use of the technology.

What's Next?

As organizations embark on their AI journey, governance readiness becomes a critical factor in ensuring the successful adoption and implementation of AI technologies. By establishing a comprehensive framework that addresses ethical considerations, legal compliance, risk management, and stakeholder engagement, organizations can navigate the complex landscape of AI with confidence and integrity.

Looking ahead to the next chapter, "Part III: How AI Technology Architecture Affects Change Success," we will explore the critical role of technology architecture in driving the effectiveness of AI-powered change initiatives.

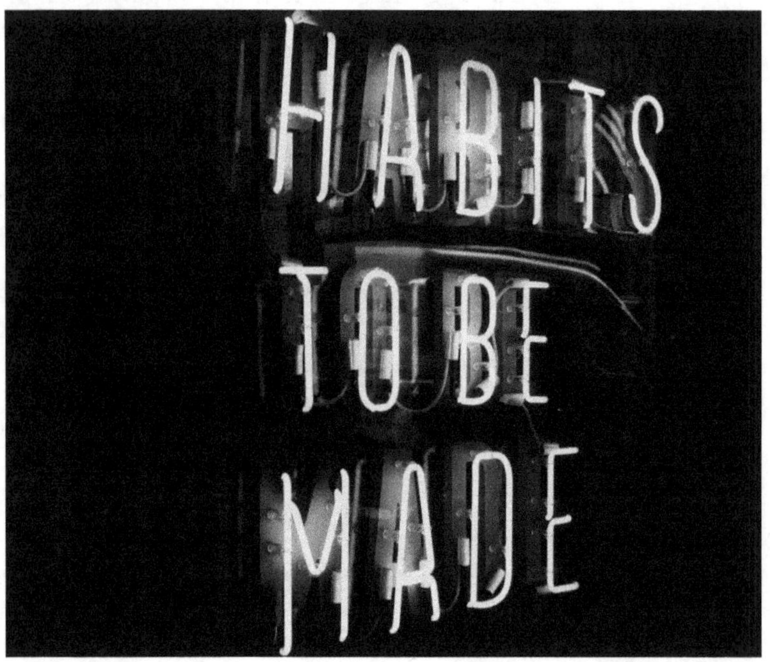
HABITS
TO BE
MADE

Part III:
How AI Technology Architecture Affects Change Success

The Change Effectiveness Equation, represented as QxA = E, is a concise mathematical formula that encapsulates the success of any change initiative within an organization. This equation highlights the crucial relationship between the Quality (Q) of the change being implemented and the Acceptance (A) it receives from stakeholders. The product of these two factors ultimately determines the Effectiveness (E) of the change.

When considering the implementation of AI-powered systems and solutions, several key components directly influence their acceptance within an organization. These components are particularly significant during the early stages of the organization's AI journey, such as the Proof of Concept stage. As the organization progresses and matures, these components will evolve and adapt accordingly.

It is important to recognize that the adoption of new technology, such as AI, may present challenges for organizations with diverse IT architectures. Achieving optimal IT Maturity is a gradual process that requires time and effort. During this transitional period, organizations may need to rely more heavily on external vendors and resources while their internal IT teams acquire the necessary knowledge and skills to effectively manage and maintain the AI-powered systems.

As the organization's IT Maturity increases, the reliance on external support will likely decrease, allowing for a more seamless integration of AI solutions into the existing infrastructure. This progression enables the organization to fully harness the potential of AI and drive meaningful change across various aspects of their operations.

CATEGORY	COMPONENT	Proof of Concept (Experiments)	Quick Wins (Employee Tasks)	Changes (Single Department Processes)	Cross Functional (Multi-Department Processes)	Transformational (New Business)
TECHNOLOGY	Data	●	●	●	●	●
	Architecture	●	●	●	●	●
	Security	●	●	●	●	●
	Vendor Standards	●	●	●	●	●
	IT Maturity				●	●

CHANGE COMPLEXITY & RISK

Let's delve deeper to help you understand the importance of IT Maturity for an organization.

Data

Data serves as the bedrock upon which AI systems are built, playing a pivotal role in both the training and operational phases of AI models. The success and effectiveness of AI solutions heavily depend on the quality, quantity, and diversity of the data utilized.

High-quality data is essential for AI models to learn and make accurate predictions or decisions. The data must be relevant, reliable, and free from errors or inconsistencies. Poor quality data can lead to inaccurate results, biased outcomes, and sub-optimal performance of AI systems. Therefore, organizations must prioritize data quality and implement robust data governance practices to ensure the integrity and reliability of the data used in AI solutions.

The quantity of data is another critical factor in the development of effective AI systems. AI models require substantial amounts of data to learn patterns, relationships, and insights. Insufficient data can limit the ability of AI models to generalize and perform well in real-world scenarios. Organizations should strive to collect and curate large, diverse datasets that cover a wide range of scenarios and edge cases to enable AI models to learn comprehensively.

Diversity in data is equally important to prevent bias and ensure the AI system's ability to handle various situations. AI models trained on narrow or biased datasets may exhibit biased behavior or struggle to perform accurately in diverse contexts. Incorporating data from different sources, demographics, and domains helps AI models develop a more comprehensive understanding and make fair and unbiased decisions.

To harness the full potential of AI, organizations must prioritize access to relevant and high-quality data sets. This involves establishing efficient data pipelines, integrating data from multiple sources, and implementing secure data storage and management practices. By ensuring the availability and accessibility of valuable data assets, organizations can empower their AI systems to learn effectively and deliver accurate and reliable results.

Investing in data quality, quantity, and diversity is a critical step in building robust and effective AI solutions. Organizations that prioritize data as the foundation of their AI initiatives are well-positioned to unlock the transformative power of artificial intelligence and drive meaningful outcomes across various domains.

Important Considerations for Leaders

As a leader, it is crucial to ensure that the data used in AI initiatives is of high quality and fit for purpose. Poor quality data can lead to inaccurate insights, flawed decision-making, and sub-optimal AI performance. By educating users about warning signs of poor data quality and implementing effective feedback processes, leaders can proactively address data issues and enhance the overall success of AI projects.

- **Bias and Stereotyping:** Bias and stereotyping in data can lead to AI models that perpetuate and amplify these prejudices, resulting in unfair and discriminatory outcomes. Leaders must be vigilant in identifying and addressing various forms of bias, such as gender, racial, or cultural biases, in the data used to train AI systems. Imagine an AI recruitment tool that has learned from historical hiring data in a male-dominated industry. If left unchecked, this system may inadvertently favor male candidates, reinforcing gender disparities in the workplace.

  The consequences of biased AI can be far-reaching, impacting individual lives and perpetuating systemic inequalities. By proactively addressing bias and promoting inclusive AI development practices, organizations can harness the power of AI while ensuring equitable treatment for all individuals. It's a critical step towards building trust and driving positive change in an AI-driven world.

- **Lack of Diversity:** A lack of diversity in AI training data can severely limit a model's ability to understand and generate responses that resonate with a wide range of users. When an AI system is exposed to a narrow set of demographics, viewpoints, and writing styles, it may struggle to comprehend and appropriately engage with the rich tapestry of human experiences and expressions. Imagine an AI language model trained primarily on text data from Western sources.

  When confronted with cultural references, idioms, or writing styles from other parts of the world, this model may falter, generating responses that are tone-deaf, insensitive, or simply irrelevant. The consequences can be significant, ranging from miscommunication and user frustration to the reinforcement of cultural biases and the exclusion of underrepresented voices. To address this challenge, leaders must prioritize diversity in data collection, actively seeking out and incorporating a wide range of perspectives and experiences.

By exposing AI models to diversity, we can create systems that are more inclusive, adaptable, and equipped to serve the needs of a global user base. Embracing diversity in AI is not just a technical imperative; it's a reflection of our shared humanity and a step towards building a more connected and understanding world.

- **Outdated Information:** In the fast-paced world of AI, outdated information can be a silent killer, undermining the reliability and effectiveness of even the most sophisticated models. As fields like medicine, technology, and social sciences continue to evolve at breakneck speed, the data used to train AI systems can quickly become stale, leading to potentially dangerous consequences.

Imagine an AI medical assistant trained on datasets from a decade ago. Unaware of the latest breakthroughs, this system may provide outdated and potentially harmful recommendations to patients, putting lives at risk. The cost of using obsolete data is not just measured in bytes, but in the trust and well-being of those who rely on AI for critical decisions. Leaders must ensure that their teams are relentless in their pursuit of up-to-date information, continuously refreshing datasets to keep pace with the latest advancements.

By ensuring that AI models are trained on the most current and relevant data, we can unlock their true potential to drive innovation, improve outcomes, and shape a better future. In the age of AI, the currency of knowledge is not just in its depth, but in its freshness—a reminder that the pursuit of progress is an ongoing journey, not a destination.

- **Inaccuracies and Errors:** In the world of AI, inaccuracies and errors can undermine the credibility and usefulness of even the most advanced models. Leaders must be the guardians of data integrity, ensuring that AI is built upon a foundation of accurate and error-free data.

- **Inappropriate or Sensitive Content:** Inappropriate and sensitive content in training data can poison AI models, leading them to perpetuate harm and offense. Leaders must be the ethical compass, vigilantly screening datasets and instilling a culture of responsibility and respect.

- **Overfitting to Specific Sources:** Overfitting to specific sources can limit an AI's ability to generalize and adapt. Leaders must be the architects of diversity, curating datasets that span a wide range of domains, styles, and cultural contexts.

- **Lack of Contextual or Domain-Specific Data:** The absence of contextual or domain-specific data can render specialized AI ineffective. Leaders must be the curators of context, collaborating with experts and sourcing specialized datasets to create truly insightful AI systems.

- **Imbalanced Data:** Imbalanced data can skew an AI's understanding, leading to biased and distorted outputs. Leaders must be the stewards of balance, carefully curating datasets to ensure fair representation of diverse topics and viewpoints.

- **Data Duplication:** Data duplication can trap AI models in a loop of overfitting and stagnation. Leaders must be the guardians of data hygiene, implementing deduplication processes and regularly auditing datasets for redundancy.

Important Considerations for Leaders

Here are several steps that leaders can take to address these issues effectively:

- **Implement an Issue Reporting Process:** Design a process to record examples of inadequate responses. Include details such as the nature of the query, the problematic response, and why the response was unsatisfactory. This documentation is crucial for providing clear feedback to the developers or the team responsible for the AI.

- **Risk Management:** Integrate these issues into governance. Understand how they impact operations and work with governance readiness stakeholders to develop plans to mitigate potential negative consequences.

- **Educate Users:** Make sure that users of the AI understand its limitations. Users should be aware that the AI might produce biased or inaccurate responses and should be trained on how to recognize and report these issues.

- **Custom Training or Tuning:** It may be possible to fine-tune the AI with additional training data that addresses the specific shortcomings. The developers will execute this process.

- **Diversify AI Resources:** If the issues are recurrent and severe, developers may consider using multiple AI systems or resources to cross-check information and responses. This can help mitigate the risk of relying on a single source that may have inherent biases or limitations.

- **Implement Oversight Mechanisms:** Promote internal review processes where responses from the AI, especially those used in critical or public-facing scenarios, are reviewed by human experts before use.

- **Stay Informed About Updates and Communicate to Users:** AI models are often updated to address issues like biases and inaccuracies. Stay informed about updates and improvements to the AI, understand how they might impact its performance, and ensure the updates are being communicated.

- **Review and Adjust Usage Policies if Needed:** If you're using the AI within your organization, review your usage policies. Ensure that users are aware of the potential limitations and issues with the AI's responses. Confirm guidelines on how to use the AI responsibly, especially in sensitive contexts.

- **Consider Collaborating With AI Ethics Experts:** For complex or sensitive issues, consider consulting with experts in AI ethics or related fields to reinforce governance readiness. They can provide valuable insights into managing the ethical challenges associated with AI systems.

Architecture

A well-designed technology architecture ensures seamless integration of AI into existing systems, supporting efficient data flow crucial for AI functionalities. It determines the organization's ability to scale AI solutions, maintain system interoperability, and manage data effectively. Essentially, the robustness and adaptability of the technological infrastructure dictate how smoothly AI initiatives can be implemented and scaled, impacting the speed and effectiveness of AI adoption, and ultimately influencing the organization's capacity to harness the full potential of AI technologies in alignment with its strategic goals.

Alignment With Business Strategy

An effective technology architecture for AI should be closely aligned with the organization's overall business strategy. This alignment ensures that AI initiatives directly support business goals, such as improving customer experience, optimizing operations, or innovating products and services. When AI is integrated in a way that complements and advances these strategic objectives, it becomes a powerful tool for achieving organizational success. Below are a few examples:

- **Improving Customer Experience:** A retail company aims to enhance its customer experience. By aligning its technology architecture with this goal, it integrates AI-powered chatbots into its customer service platform. These chatbots use natural language processing to provide quick and accurate responses to customer inquiries, improving response times and customer satisfaction. Additionally, AI-driven recommendation systems are implemented on the company's e-commerce platform, offering personalized product suggestions based on customer browsing and purchase history, thus enhancing the shopping experience.

- **Optimizing Operations:** A manufacturing firm seeks to optimize its operations for efficiency and cost reduction. Its technology architecture is designed to support AI initiatives like predictive maintenance. Here, AI algorithms analyze data from sensors on equipment to predict when maintenance is needed, reducing downtime and maintenance costs. Additionally, AI-driven logistics optimization tools are used to streamline supply chain processes, enhancing inventory management and reducing waste.

- **Innovating Products and Services:** A healthcare provider focuses on innovating its services for better patient care. The organization's technology architecture supports the integration of AI in diagnostic tools. For instance, AI algorithms are used to analyze medical images more quickly and accurately than traditional methods, aiding in early and precise diagnosis of diseases. Furthermore, AI-powered personalized treatment plans are developed, using patient data to tailor treatments to individual needs, improving patient outcomes.

- **Enhancing Marketing Strategies:** A digital marketing agency aims to deliver more targeted and effective campaigns. By aligning its technology architecture with this goal, AI is used to analyze large datasets of consumer behavior. This enables the creation of highly targeted marketing campaigns, using insights from AI to identify effective channels and messages for different customer segments, leading to higher conversion rates and better ROI on marketing spend.

- **Financial Risk Management:** A bank focuses on enhancing its risk management capabilities. Its technology architecture supports the integration of AI for credit scoring models, which use machine learning to analyze customer data and predict creditworthiness more accurately. This reduces the risk of loan defaults. Additionally, AI is used for fraud detection, identifying unusual patterns in transactions that may indicate fraudulent activity, thereby protecting both the bank and its customers.

The alignment of technology architecture with business goals is crucial for the successful adoption and utilization of AI. Without this alignment, organizations risk inefficiency, wasted resources, and a failure to leverage AI for strategic advantage.

Scalability and Flexibility

A key aspect of AI-ready architecture is its scalability and flexibility. As the organization grows and its needs evolve, the architecture should be able to scale accordingly. This includes the ability to handle increasing volumes of data, more complex AI models, and a growing number of AI applications. Flexible architecture allows for the addition of new technologies and methodologies without major overhauls, thereby reducing future costs and disruption.

Data Integration and Management

As already discussed, AI requires high-quality, accessible data. A robust technology architecture facilitates the integration of disparate data sources and ensures consistent, reliable data management. This includes proper data governance, quality control, and secure data storage and access. Well-managed data is crucial for training accurate AI models and for providing the ongoing data inputs needed for AI systems to function effectively in a dynamic business environment.

Interoperability With Existing Systems

Integrating AI into the existing IT landscape without causing disruptions is a significant challenge. The technology architecture should support interoperability, allowing AI systems to connect with legacy systems, databases, and software applications. This ensures continuity in business processes while introducing AI capabilities, thereby minimizing resistance to change and ensuring smoother adoption.

Compliance and Security

As AI systems often process sensitive data, the architecture must be designed with a strong emphasis on security and compliance. This includes adherence to data protection regulations, implementation of robust cybersecurity measures, and ensuring that AI systems are transparent and accountable. Security will be further discussed in depth in the next section.

Important Considerations for Leaders

There are indicators that can help leaders determine if adoption risks may occur resulting from an organization's Technology Architecture Readiness for AI.

- **Misaligned Priorities:** Misaligned priorities can derail AI projects, turning them into flashy but useless props. Leaders must choreograph AI investments to focus on critical areas driving organizational success, ensuring each move is purposeful and strategic in addressing key business challenges. Without alignment, AI projects risk becoming wasteful sideshows, squandering resources and opportunities better directed towards impactful endeavors.

- **Integration Challenges:** AI solutions that fail to integrate with existing systems can grind organizational machinery to a halt. Isolated AI tools become bottlenecks, slowing down processes they were meant to streamline. Leaders must be master mechanics, designing AI architectures that fit smoothly into existing frameworks, eliminating friction and enabling harmonious interplay between AI and digital counterparts. Without integration, AI risks becoming a clunky appendage rather than a seamless enhancement.

- **Inefficient Use of Data:** Data is the lifeblood of AI, but when technology architecture fails to support AI's data needs, it becomes a clogged artery starving the system. Poor data quality, inaccessibility, and mismanagement render even advanced AI tools impotent. Leaders must be data doctors, diagnosing and treating data pipeline ailments to ensure a steady, healthy information flow to AI algorithms. Without data efficiency, AI becomes a brilliant mind trapped in a dysfunctional body.

- **Increased Costs and Delays:** When AI projects don't line up with business needs, they can get stuck in a trap of rising costs and delays. These projects can waste time and money by going in the wrong direction. Leaders must act as guides, always making sure AI efforts are heading towards the right goal. If AI projects aren't aligned with the business, they might end up being costly and time-consuming without ever reaching their full potential.

- **Risk of Obsolescence:** In the fast-moving world of AI, not keeping up with current and future business goals can make an organization fall behind. As technology changes quickly, AI solutions that aren't made to adapt and stay relevant become outdated and can't keep up with new demands. Leaders need to be forward-thinkers, predicting how the industry will change and guiding AI plans to stay ahead. If AI isn't aligned with the future, it might become an old tool that holds the organization back while others move forward boldly.

- **Reduced Engagement and Adoption:** In the big picture of putting AI into action, if employees don't get on board and use it, even the best plans can fail quietly. When AI tools don't get people excited and interested, they end up being ignored and forgotten. Leaders need to be like movie directors, creating a story that shows how great AI can be and getting everyone to play their part. If the people aren't bought in, AI might just become a side story that never reaches its big, world-changing ending.

Security

Security is a paramount concern when implementing AI systems within an organization, as these systems often handle sensitive data and play critical roles in decision-making processes. Ensuring the security of AI systems is essential to maintain trust, protect sensitive information, and comply with relevant regulations and standards.

One of the primary security considerations in AI is protecting data from unauthorized access. It is crucial to implement strong access controls, such as role-based access, multi-factor authentication, and encryption, to ensure that only authorized personnel can access the data used by AI systems. This helps prevent data breaches, unauthorized modifications, and misuse of sensitive information.

Data integrity is another critical aspect of AI security. AI models rely on the accuracy and reliability of the data they are trained on and the data they process during operation. Any tampering, corruption, or manipulation of data can lead to incorrect predictions, biased outcomes, and compromised decision-making. Implementing robust data validation, integrity checks, and version control mechanisms helps ensure the integrity of data throughout the AI lifecycle.

Safeguarding against malicious AI use is also a significant concern. As AI systems become more powerful and autonomous, there is a risk of these systems being exploited for malicious purposes, such as generating fake content, conducting cyber attacks, or manipulating public opinion. Organizations must implement stringent security measures, such as input validation, output filtering, and anomaly detection, to prevent the misuse of AI systems and mitigate potential harm.

Regular security audits, penetration testing, and vulnerability assessments help identify and address potential security weaknesses in AI systems.

Investing in robust security measures is essential for the successful deployment and operation of AI systems. By prioritizing data protection, ensuring data integrity, safeguarding against malicious use, maintaining transparency and accountability, and complying with relevant regulations, organizations can build trust in their AI systems and unlock the full potential of AI while mitigating risks and protecting sensitive information.

Important Considerations for Leaders

Leaders play an essential role in ensuring the effective and secure implementation of AI systems within an organization. This involves educating users, maintaining robust security measures, and collaborating with IT and Governance.

- **Access Controls:** leaders must educate users on access types, provisioning processes, and rationales for AI systems. This includes user authentication, role-based access, and permission management to prevent unauthorized access to sensitive data.

- **Data Encryption and Anonymization:** Sensitive data, including personal and proprietary information, must be encrypted. leaders should promote data anonymization techniques for external GenAI applications to protect privacy while leveraging AI capabilities.

- **Cybersecurity Measures:** Leaders should stay updated on the latest cybersecurity trends and threats. Firewalls, intrusion detection systems, and regular security audits protect against external threats like hacking or malicious AI use.

- **Emergency Response Plan:** Leaders should be aware of emergency response plans for potential security breaches. This includes immediate containment steps, investigation procedures, and data recovery strategies. Communication procedures and end-user roles may require support.

- **Intellectual Property Protection:** AI systems, especially GenAI, handle sensitive and proprietary data, necessitating robust security protocols for both internal and external applications. For internal GenAI use, access controls ensure only authorized personnel can access IP-related data. AI auditing systems track IP usage and modification, providing an audit trail for unauthorized use. For external GenAI use, like OpenAI's ChatGPT, data anonymization mitigates IP exposure risks. Removing identifiable details protects sensitive IP while allowing the use of external GenAI tools.

Vendor Standards

AI Vendor Standards are essentially focused on a robust framework for evaluating and selecting the right AI technology vendors for an organization. This process is multi-dimensional and includes several key aspects:

- **Assessing Technology Reliability:** Evaluating the consistency and performance of the AI technology under various conditions is crucial. It's important to consider how the technology has performed in real-world applications, examining metrics such as accuracy, precision, recall, and error rates. Additionally, understanding the adaptability of the AI under different scenarios can provide insights into its robustness and versatility.

- **Security Evaluation:** Given the sensitive nature of data involved in AI systems, assessing a vendor's commitment to data protection regulations such as GDPR and CCPA is essential. This includes evaluating the robustness of their encryption methods and their protocols for preventing data breaches. Vendors should have strong incident response plans, regular security audits, and diligent staff training programs to ensure comprehensive data security.

- **Scalability Consideration:** The AI solution should not just meet your current needs but also be scalable to accommodate future growth. This involves evaluating the technology's ability to handle increasing amounts of data or transactions without a significant drop in performance. Additionally, it is important to assess the vendor's capacity to support such growth through technical assistance and resources, ensuring the solution remains future-proof.

- **Compatibility With Existing Systems:** Ensuring seamless integration with your existing IT infrastructure is vital. The new AI technology should integrate well with current hardware, software, and data formats. The ease of integration can be assessed by reviewing API documentation, SDKs, and other integration tools provided by the vendor.

- **Vendor's Track Record and Support Capabilities:** Reviewing the vendor's previous projects, client testimonials, and case studies can provide valuable insights into their reliability. Additionally, the quality of their customer support, including responsiveness, expertise, and the availability of training and resources, is crucial for ongoing success.

- **Alignment With Business Goals:** The AI solution should support and enhance your strategic objectives. This means the technology should not only solve current problems but also contribute to long-term goals such as improving customer experience, increasing operational efficiency, and driving innovation. Defining and measuring key performance indicators can help track the AI solution's impact on these goals.

- **Cost-Effectiveness:** While it's important not to compromise on quality, evaluating the cost implications of the AI solution is essential. This includes not only the initial investment but also the long-term costs associated with maintenance, updates, training, and scaling. Conducting a Total Cost of Ownership (TCO) analysis and assessing the potential return on investment can provide a clearer financial picture.

- **Ethical Considerations:** Ensuring that AI solutions adhere to ethical standards, including fairness, transparency, and accountability, is crucial. It's particularly important in areas like data usage and decision-making processes. Vendors should provide clear notices and terms for non-expert users to help build trust in AI. Methods to ensure ethical considerations include:

  - **Model Interpretability:** Designing AI models to be inherently understandable is key. Simpler models like decision trees or linear regression naturally lend themselves to this approach, along with thorough documentation and user guides to facilitate understanding.

  - **Post-Hoc Explanation:** For more complex models like neural networks, post-hoc techniques provide explanations after a decision is made. Methods like LIME (Local Interpretable Model-Agnostic Explanations) and SHAP (SHapley Additive exPlanations) break down and illustrate how a model arrived at a particular outcome, offering user-friendly tools for generating and understanding these explanations.

  - **Visualization Tools:** Visualization is powerful for explainable AI, providing more intuitive insights into complex processes. Tools like heat maps, graphs, interactive dashboards, and other visual aids help illustrate the features influencing AI decisions.

- **Regulatory Compliance:** To avoid legal complications and ensure ethical use of AI technologies, vendors should comply with relevant industry regulations and standards, such as ISO/IEC 27001 for information security management. Regular audits should be conducted to ensure ongoing compliance with these regulatory standards.

Important Considerations for Leaders

There are various ways to leverage this information:

- **Framework for Evaluating Tools:** This framework can be used by leaders to assess tools that facilitate change. For example, they may engage a vendor whose tool automates training development.

- **Discussion Points for Vendor Selection:** These points can help understand the selection process and the final scoring behind vendor selection. Areas that scored weaker may require additional focus or efforts to drive change.

IT Maturity

IT Maturity is a critical factor in the successful implementation and long-term sustainability of AI initiatives within an organization. It refers to the readiness and capability of the IT department to effectively adopt, integrate, and maintain AI technologies. Achieving a high level of IT Maturity requires a combination of technical expertise, resources, and ongoing skill development.

This concept encompasses several key dimensions:

Processes and Practices

Well-defined, documented, and implemented IT processes are crucial for successful AI adoption. Leaders should ensure that IT service management, project management, and quality assurance practices are robust and adaptable to accommodate AI-specific requirements.

People and Skills

The expertise and proficiency of IT staff play a vital role in AI readiness. Leaders should focus on developing and nurturing the technical skills of IT personnel, providing training opportunities, and fostering a culture of continuous learning to keep pace with the rapidly evolving AI landscape.

Alignment With Business Goals

Effective alignment between IT strategy and overall business strategy is essential for realizing the full potential of AI. Leaders must ensure that IT initiatives, including AI projects, are closely integrated with business objectives, driving innovation and contributing to tangible business outcomes.

Governance and Risk Management

Robust governance and risk management mechanisms are critical for the responsible and compliant implementation of AI. Leaders should collaborate with IT to establish governance frameworks that align AI investments with business objectives, manage risks effectively, and ensure compliance with relevant laws and regulations.

Performance Measurement

Measuring and tracking IT performance using well-defined metrics and key performance indicators is crucial for informed decision-making and continuous improvement. Leaders should work with IT to establish performance measurement systems that provide insights into the effectiveness and efficiency of AI initiatives, enabling data-driven optimization and refinement.

In the context of AI adoption, organizations with a higher level of IT maturity are generally better equipped to integrate AI solutions effectively. They tend to have the necessary infrastructure, skilled personnel, robust processes, and a strategic alignment that enables them to leverage AI technologies to enhance business operations and drive innovation.

GenAI is still new and evolving fast so IT Maturity is expected to take time to develop as shown in the Technology Readiness graphic at the beginning of this section.

Evolution of IT Maturity With AI Projects

Based on an organization's progression through various project types—acknowledging the increase in change complexity and risk—let's examine how IT Maturity might evolve with each type of AI project.

Proof of Concept (Experiments)

The Proof of Concept phase is crucial for organizations exploring the integration of AI technologies. During this phase, various aspects are tested and evaluated to determine feasibility and potential impact. The following key components are essential to a successful PoC.

Technology and Infrastructure

Category	Details
Investment in AI Technologies	Acquisition of new AI tools and software, including machine learning frameworks, natural language processing tools, and other AI-based applications.
Infrastructure Setup	Opting for cloud-based AI services (AWS, Google Cloud, Azure) to ensure scalability and flexibility tailored to project needs.
Data Management Systems	Setting up efficient data collection, storage, and processing systems such as databases, data lakes, and data warehouses to handle large volumes of data.

Computational Resources	Utilizing high-performance computing resources, including GPUs and TPUs, for effective processing and analysis of large datasets.

Processes and Practices

Category	Details
Agile Methodologies	Emphasis on iterative development, rapid prototyping, and continuous feedback, allowing teams to adapt quickly to new findings.
Rapid Prototyping	Developing quick prototypes to test hypotheses and validate assumptions early, identifying potential issues and refining solutions pre-implementation.
Experimental Mindset	Fostering a learning and innovation environment where failure is seen as a learning opportunity.
Testing and Validation	Establishing rigorous testing and validation processes (e.g., cross-validation, A/B testing, performance benchmarking) to ensure accuracy and reliability of AI models.

People and Skills

Category	Details
Training and Development	Providing initial AI and data analytics training through workshops, online courses, and hands-on sessions led by experts.
Skill Development	Leveraging the PoC phase to develop AI literacy and technical skills, enabling IT teams to work with AI tools, interpret data, and build models.
Collaboration and Cross-Functional Teams	Involving cross-functional teams (data scientists, engineers, domain experts, and business analysts) to foster diverse perspectives and enhance problem-solving.
Knowledge Sharing	Utilizing internal seminars, documentation, and collaboration platforms to disseminate learnings across the organization.

Alignment With Business Goals

Category	Details
Strategic Planning	Understanding how AI aligns with and supports business goals by identifying relevant KPIs and metrics.
Use Case Identification	Identifying and prioritizing specific AI use cases based on potential business value to focus efforts on impactful projects.

Stakeholder Engagement	Ensuring alignment with business needs and securing necessary support by engaging key stakeholders, including executives, managers, and end-users.
Long-Term Vision	Using insights from PoC experiments to inform the long-term AI strategy and roadmap, guiding future investments and initiatives.

Governance and Risk Management

Category	**Details**
Risk Assessment	Developing initial frameworks for managing AI-related risks, such as data privacy issues, ethical concerns, and biases in AI models.
Data Privacy and Security	Implementing measures like encryption, access controls, and compliance with regulations (GDPR, CCPA) to ensure data privacy and security.
Ethical Considerations	Establishing ethical guidelines for responsible and transparent AI use, focusing on fairness, accountability, and transparency.
Regulatory Compliance	Ensuring compliance with industry standards and regulations by understanding requirements and implementing relevant practices.

Performance Measurement

Category	**Details**
Defining Metrics	Establishing clear metrics for evaluating AI experiments, including accuracy, precision, recall, and other relevant performance indicators.
Feasibility Analysis	Assessing the technical viability, resource requirements, and potential ROI of AI solutions.
Business Value Assessment	Measuring the potential business value of AI experiments in terms of operational efficiency, cost savings, revenue generation, and customer satisfaction.
Continuous Monitoring and Improvement	Continuously monitoring performance and using insights to make iterative improvements, ensuring optimized AI solutions that deliver maximum value.

Quick Wins (Employee Tasks)

The Quick Wins phase focuses on identifying and implementing small, manageable AI projects that can deliver immediate value. During this phase, specific tasks are assigned to employees to ensure rapid deployment and early success. These tasks are designed to demonstrate the tangible benefits of AI technology, build momentum, and foster a culture of innovation within the organization.

Technology and Infrastructure

Category	Details
Integration of Specific AI Tools	Identify and implement advanced AI tools tailored to organizational needs, ensuring seamless integration into the current tech stack.
Enhancement of Existing Infrastructure	Upgrade and optimize existing infrastructure to support new AI applications, including increasing server capacity, enhancing network capabilities, or incorporating cloud-based solutions.
Maintenance and Updates	Establish a regular maintenance schedule to keep AI tools and supporting infrastructure up-to-date with the latest features and security patches.

Processes and Practices

Category	Details
AI-Driven Workflow Refinement	Analyze current workflows to identify areas where AI can streamline processes, reduce manual effort, and improve efficiency. Implement AI solutions in these areas.
Seamless AI Integration	Develop strategies to embed AI technologies into daily tasks without disrupting existing workflows, including training sessions, user-friendly interfaces, and robust support systems.
Monitoring and Evaluation	Create a framework for continuously monitoring the effectiveness of AI-driven workflows and making iterative improvements based on feedback and performance metrics.

People and Skills

Category	Details
Training Programs	Offer more comprehensive training programs to increase AI literacy among employees, including hands-on workshops, online courses, and certification programs.
Skill Development	Encourage employees to develop new AI-related skills, such as data analysis, and AI ethics, providing resources for learning.

Adoption Facilitation	Implement strategies to ease the transition to AI tools, including change management practices, user support hotlines, and internal champions to advocate for AI adoption.

Alignment With Business Goals

Category	Details
Efficiency Improvement	Conduct pilot projects to showcase the direct benefits of AI in enhancing operational efficiency, documenting and sharing success stories to build a compelling case for further AI integration.
Strategic Roadmap	Align AI initiatives with the organization's long-term business goals, developing a strategic roadmap that outlines how AI can contribute to achieving these objectives.
Stakeholder Engagement	Regularly engage with key stakeholders, including senior management, to ensure alignment and gain support for AI initiatives, presenting data-driven insights to demonstrate the tangible benefits of AI.

Governance and Risk Management

Category	Details
Policy Development	Develop and implement policies for responsible AI use, addressing data privacy, ethical considerations, and compliance with relevant regulations.
Risk Assessment	Conduct thorough risk assessments to identify potential risks associated with AI implementation, developing mitigation strategies to address these risks.
Continuous Improvement	Establish a governance framework that includes continuous monitoring and evaluation of AI use, ensuring adherence to policies and making improvements as needed.

Performance Measurement

Category	Details
Operational Metrics Adaptation	Identify key performance indicators to measure the impact of AI on employee productivity and task efficiency, such as time saved, error reduction, and output quality.
Regular Reporting	Develop a reporting system to track and communicate the performance of AI initiatives, regularly sharing insights with stakeholders to maintain transparency.

Feedback Loop	Create a feedback loop to gather input from employees on the effectiveness of AI tools and processes, using this feedback to make data-driven adjustments and improvements.

Changes (Single Department Processes)

The Changes phase targets the optimization of processes within a single department through the integration of AI technologies. During this phase, specific departmental processes are analyzed and modified to enhance efficiency and effectiveness. This focused approach allows for controlled experimentation and improvement, providing clear insights into the benefits of AI and creating a foundation for broader organizational changes.

Technology and Infrastructure

Category	**Details**
Implementation of Department-Specific AI Solutions	Each department adopts tailored AI technologies catering to their unique operational needs, identifying specific challenges and opportunities, and selecting the best-fit AI tools.
Advanced Integration With Departmental Systems	Technical adjustments to ensure seamless interaction between new AI tools and existing systems, including hardware upgrades, software configuration refinements, and establishing robust data pipelines.

Processes and Practices

Category	Details
Process Re-Engineering	Revisit and redesign traditional workflows to fully exploit AI capabilities, automating repetitive tasks, introducing predictive analytics for decision-making, and creating more dynamic and adaptable processes.
Innovative Workflows	Foster innovation by enabling departments to operate more efficiently and responsively, using AI-driven systems to provide real-time insights for quicker and more informed decisions.

People and Skills

Category	Details
Development of Specialized AI Skills	Encourage staff within each department to acquire skills specific to the AI tools they will be using through formal training programs, workshops, and continuous learning opportunities.
Domain-Specific AI Expertise	Employees focus on how AI applies to their particular field, with IT teams delving into AI for customer analytics, predictive financial modeling, etc.

Alignment With Business Goals

Category	Details
Clarification of AI's Role	Clearly define AI's role in achieving departmental objectives, ensuring each department understands how AI contributes to their goals, whether it's improving efficiency, enhancing customer satisfaction, or driving revenue growth.
Alignment With Broader Business Strategies	Align AI initiatives with the organization's overall strategic vision, with departments working collaboratively to ensure AI-driven projects support and amplify the company's broader business objectives.

Governance and Risk Management

Category	Details
Functionally-Specific Governance Issues	Address governance issues related to AI within departments, ensuring compliance with industry standards and regulations, and setting up protocols for ethical AI use, data privacy, and security.
Risk Management	Identify and manage potential risks associated with AI deployment proactively, developing risk mitigation strategies tailored to their specific AI applications.

Performance Measurement

Category	Details
Evolution of KPIs	Update Key Performance Indicators to reflect the impact of AI on departmental processes, supplementing traditional KPIs with new metrics measuring AI-driven enhancements such as process efficiency, accuracy, and innovation.
Continuous Monitoring and Improvement	Continuously monitor AI performance, using data-driven insights to refine processes and improve outcomes, establishing feedback loops to ensure ongoing optimization and adjustment of AI tools and strategies.

Cross-Functional (Multi-Department Processes)

The Cross-Functional phase aims to integrate AI technologies across multiple departments to streamline and enhance inter-departmental processes. During this phase, workflows that span various functions are examined and re-engineered to leverage AI capabilities. This holistic approach fosters better collaboration, ensures consistency, and drives significant improvements in overall organizational performance by breaking down silos and optimizing end-to-end processes.

Technology and Infrastructure

Category	Details
Evolution of Infrastructure	Robust IT infrastructure to support sophisticated AI technologies, including scalable cloud solutions, high-performance computing resources, and secure data storage systems.
Integration Efforts	Seamless integration of software systems and databases across departments, using sophisticated middleware, APIs, and ETL processes to ensure smooth data flow.
Data Management	Efficient data management practices, including data cleaning, normalization, and ensuring compliance with data governance policies.

Processes and Practices

Category	Details
Collaborative Workflows	Establishing clear workflows that facilitate communication and task management across departments to support AI projects needing input from multiple departments.
Integrated Processes	Standardizing processes across departments to ensure consistency in AI tools and methodologies application, ensuring reliable and comparable outputs.

People and Skills

Category	Details
Training Programs	Investing in comprehensive training programs to upskill employees in AI-related fields, including technical skills and understanding AI's impact on business functions.
Interdisciplinary Teams	Creating teams combining technical experts, domain specialists, and business analysts to foster a more holistic approach to AI projects.
Culture of Learning	Encouraging a culture that values continuous learning and curiosity, helping employees stay updated with the latest AI developments and applications.

Alignment With Business Goals

Category	Details
Strategic Planning	Continuously aligning AI initiatives with the organization's strategic objectives, ensuring ongoing communication between AI teams and business leadership.
Value Proposition	Clearly defining the value proposition of AI projects to secure stakeholder buy-in and focus on delivering tangible business benefits.

Feedback Loops	Establishing feedback mechanisms for continual assessment of AI initiatives, ensuring alignment with evolving business goals.

Governance and Risk Management

Category	Details
Advanced Governance Models	Updating the governance framework with policies, procedures, and guidelines for AI use, addressing data privacy, ethical considerations, and regulation compliance.
Risk Assessment	Conducting regular risk assessments to identify potential AI deployment issues, including technical risks and operational risks.
Mitigation Strategies	Developing mitigation strategies, including contingency plans and robust security measures, to manage identified risks effectively.

Performance Measurement

Category	Details
Expanded Metrics	Developing new metrics to specifically measure the effectiveness and efficiency of AI-driven processes, as traditional metrics may not fully capture AI's impact.

Continuous Monitoring	Ongoing performance monitoring using real-time analytics and regular performance reviews to identify areas of value and improvement.
ROI Evaluation	Evaluating AI projects' return on investment, considering not only financial metrics but also improvements in process efficiency, customer satisfaction, and innovation capacity.

Transformational (New Business)

The Transformational phase focuses on leveraging AI technologies to create entirely new business models and opportunities. During this phase, organizations explore innovative ways to harness AI for developing new products, services, or markets. This transformative approach aims to redefine the business landscape, drive significant competitive advantages, and position the organization as a leader in the AI-driven economy.

Technology and Infrastructure

Category	**Details**
Adopting Advanced AI Technologies	Implementing cutting-edge AI technologies such as machine learning, natural language processing, and computer vision to drive innovation.
Modernizing IT Infrastructure	Upgrading existing IT infrastructure to handle sophisticated AI applications' computational requirements.

Cloud Computing Solutions	Utilizing cloud platforms to provide scalable and flexible resources for AI development and deployment.

Processes and Practices

Category	**Details**
Automating Routine Tasks	Using AI to automate repetitive and mundane tasks, increasing efficiency and reducing human error.
AI-Driven Decision Making	Implementing AI algorithms to analyze vast amounts of data and provide insights for strategic decision-making.
Agile Methodologies	Adopting agile practices to enable rapid development and deployment of AI solutions, ensuring quick adaptation to changing market demands.

People and Skills

Category	**Details**
Comprehensive Training Programs	Developing training modules to educate employees about AI technologies and their applications within the business.
Cross-Functional Teams	Encouraging collaboration between AI experts and other departments to foster a holistic approach to AI integration.

Continuous Learning Culture	Promoting a culture of continuous learning and development to keep pace with rapid advancements in AI.
Talent Acquisition	Attracting and retaining top talent with expertise in AI, data science, and related fields to drive innovation.

Alignment With Business Goals

Category	**Details**
Strategic AI Roadmap	AI becomes a core component of the organization's strategic vision and competitive advantage. A clear roadmap aligning AI initiatives with the organization's long-term goals and objectives should be developed.

Governance and Risk Management

Category	**Details**
Ethical AI Practices	Ensuring AI applications are developed and deployed ethically, focusing on fairness, transparency, and accountability.
Regulatory Compliance	Adhering to relevant laws and regulations governing AI usage, including data privacy and security standards.
Risk Mitigation	Identifying potential risks associated with AI, such as algorithmic bias and data

Plans	breaches, and developing mitigation strategies.
AI Governance Framework	Establishing a structured framework for AI governance, including policies, procedures, and oversight mechanisms.

Performance Measurement

Category	**Details**
AI-Specific KPIs	Defining key performance indicators related to AI initiatives, such as model accuracy, processing speed, and user adoption rates.
Business Impact Metrics	Measuring AI's impact on business outcomes, including revenue growth, cost savings, and customer satisfaction.
Continuous Monitoring	Implementing systems for continuous monitoring and evaluation of AI performance, ensuring ongoing improvements.
Feedback Loops	Creating feedback mechanisms to gather user input and refine AI solutions based on real-world experiences.

Important Considerations for Leaders

By the time an organization decides to pursue cross-functional AI initiatives, it's crucial for the IT team to have reached a sufficient level of maturity to support these complex initiatives. Below are several strategies that leaders can recommend and support to mitigate the risks associated with IT maturity:

Business Needs May Require Leapfrogging to More Complex Initiatives

Leaders may be engaged to rapidly scale solutions from PoCs to full-blown Cross-Functional Projects or Transformations. In this instance, leaders can engage with IT leadership in the following ways to mitigate risks:

- **Risk Assessment and Management:** Rapid scaling can introduce various risks, including technical, operational, and cultural risks. Facilitating a thorough risk assessment and developing a risk management plan is crucial. The leader should assist in identifying potential pitfalls and put in place mitigation strategies to manage these risks proactively. This includes regular risk reviews, contingency planning, and establishing a risk response team that can act swiftly to address issues as they arise.

- **Strategic Planning:** A leader can assist in developing a comprehensive plan that includes the change management steps needed to scale from a PoC to more extensive projects. This plan should include clear milestones, timelines, and defined outcomes to ensure the transition is smooth and aligned with business objectives. Additionally, the leader should ensure that strategic planning is iterative, with regular reviews and adjustments based on project progress and feedback from stakeholders.

- **Stakeholder Engagement and Communication:** Effective communication is key. The leader should engage with stakeholders at all levels—from executive leadership to department heads and frontline employees—to understand their concerns and manage expectations, particularly around potential risks and mitigations. Regular updates through various communication channels such as meetings, newsletters, and dashboards can help maintain transparency and build trust throughout the organization.

- **Resource Allocation and Prioritization:** Scaling AI projects rapidly often requires significant resources. The leader should work closely with IT leadership to ensure that adequate resources (budget, personnel, technology) are allocated. This involves not only securing resources but also prioritizing their deployment to the most critical areas. Resource allocation should be dynamic, with the flexibility to reallocate based on changing project needs and priorities.

- **Capability Building and Training:** Scaling AI solutions requires a workforce skilled in new technologies. The leader may oversee the implementation of programs for training and upskilling employees, ensuring that the necessary skills and knowledge are disseminated throughout the organization. This can include formal training sessions, on-the-job training, and creating a knowledge-sharing culture through forums, mentorship programs, and collaborative tools.

- **Agile Implementation and Iterative Development:** Adopting an agile methodology can be beneficial in managing the uncertainties and rapid changes associated with scaling AI solutions. This approach allows for flexibility, regular feedback, and iterative development, making it easier to adapt to changing requirements and challenges. The leader should champion agile practices such as daily stand-ups, sprints, and retrospectives to maintain momentum and foster continuous improvement.

- **Cultivate a Change-Ready IT Culture:** The leader should work to foster a culture that is open to change and innovation. This involves addressing resistance, encouraging a mindset of continuous adaptability, and recognizing and rewarding flexibility and innovation. Creating an environment where employees feel safe to voice concerns and experiment with new ideas can drive a more proactive and engaged workforce, ultimately supporting smoother transitions and greater resilience in the face of change.

By engaging in these ways, leaders can ensure that the process of scaling from PoCs to larger projects is managed effectively, with risks mitigated and aligned with strategic business goals.

IT Areas May Mature at Different Paces

Depending upon the organization of the IT function, various areas may progress faster than others. For example, security may need to mature faster than infrastructure. Also, IT functions may be divisionalized, where there are dedicated leadership and support teams for specific lines of business or operations within an organization. Some may report to business line heads and others may report into global technology leadership. The challenge of varying maturation paces across different IT areas is common in organizations, especially those adopting AI.

Here's how a leader can help mitigate this challenge:

- **Holistic IT Assessment:** Conduct a comprehensive assessment of the current maturity levels of different IT areas. This assessment should consider technology, processes, people, and alignment with business goals. The leader should employ a detailed framework that evaluates readiness, identifies gaps, and maps out a maturity roadmap for each area. This roadmap will serve as a benchmark to measure progress and guide decision-making.

- **Facilitate Cross-Departmental Collaboration:** Encourage collaboration and communication between different IT areas and departments. This can help in sharing best practices, resources, and knowledge, leading to more balanced development. Facilitating regular inter-departmental meetings and workshops can be effective in this regard. The leader should also establish collaborative platforms and communities of practice where teams can regularly interact and learn from one another.

- **Resource Allocation Based on Maturity Needs:** Advocate for and assist in the allocation of resources (budget, personnel, technology) according to the maturity needs of each IT area. The leader should work closely with leadership to ensure resource distribution is equitable and strategic, focusing on areas that require the most immediate attention. This might involve temporarily reallocating resources from more mature areas to support those trailing behind.

- **Leverage External Expertise When Needed:** In cases where internal resources or knowledge are insufficient, advise on partnering with external experts or consultants.

This can provide the necessary guidance and expertise to accelerate maturity. The leader should vet and recommend reputable external partners who have a track record of success in similar environments, ensuring that their contributions are aligned with the organization's strategic goals.

- **Promote a Unified IT Culture:** Work towards creating an IT culture that values diverse maturity levels as a strength rather than a challenge. Encourage a mindset where more mature areas mentor and support less mature ones, fostering an environment of mutual learning and support. The leader should implement recognition programs that celebrate collaborative successes and create opportunities for cross-functional teams to share their achievements and learnings.

- **Customized Training and Skill Development:** Recognize that different IT areas may require varied skills and knowledge, especially in the context of AI. Implement tailored training programs for each area to address specific skill gaps. Encourage continuous learning and upskilling to keep pace with evolving AI technologies. The leader should collaborate with HR and Learning and Development teams to design and deliver training programs that are relevant, engaging, and effective.

- **Review and Adjust:** Continuously review the progress of each IT area in terms of maturity. Be ready to make strategic adjustments as necessary, based on performance, technological advancements, and changing business needs. The leader should establish regular checkpoints and performance metrics to track progress, solicit feedback, and adjust the maturity roadmap as needed to ensure alignment with overall organizational objectives.

By addressing these areas, a leader can help ensure that varying maturity levels within IT functions are effectively managed, leading to a more cohesive and capable IT organization ready to leverage AI and other advanced technologies.

Segments of the IT Function May Be Outsourced to Third Parties

Many IT departments within large organizations outsource some or significant amounts of their technology operations to partners who are tasked with maintaining and evolving their architectures. This outsourcing can include various functions such as infrastructure management, software development, and support services, among others. In these instances, a leader can play a vital role in ensuring that both internal and outsourced IT personnel mature appropriately to support AI. The role of a leader becomes crucial in navigating the complexities of integrating AI technologies, aligning diverse teams towards common objectives, and fostering a collaborative environment that can adapt to the rapid advancements in AI. Below are suggested strategies:

- **Establish Clear Communication and Goals:** Collaborate with IT leadership to implement robust communication between the organization and third-party providers. Effective communication channels are essential for ensuring that both parties are aligned in terms of goals, expectations, and progress. This alignment helps prevent misunderstandings and facilitates smoother project execution. Regular meetings and updates can help maintain this alignment, providing opportunities to reassess and realign as necessary. The aim is to create a transparent and continuous dialogue that keeps both internal and external teams informed and engaged, ultimately driving the successful integration of AI.

- **Support Strong Partnerships:** Foster a relationship with third-party providers that goes beyond a mere vendor-client dynamic. This involves nurturing partnerships where the third-party is seen as an integral part of the team, contributing to long-term success rather than just delivering short-term results. A partnership approach encourages a deeper level of commitment and collaboration, which can lead to more innovative and effective integration of AI technologies. Building strong partnerships requires effort and investment in relationship-building activities, mutual respect, and a shared vision for success.

- **Cultural Integration:** Work on integrating the third-party teams into the organization's IT culture. Cultural integration is key to creating a more cohesive environment that is conducive to successful AI integration. This can involve sharing corporate values, norms, and practices with third-party teams to ensure they feel like a part of the organization's fabric. A unified culture can lead to better teamwork, higher morale, and a more seamless integration process, as all members are working towards the same goals in a harmonious manner.

- **Ensure Alignment With Business Objectives:** Work closely with third-party providers to ensure their efforts are in line with the organization's overall business strategy and AI objectives. This includes involving them in strategic discussions and planning sessions, ensuring they understand the broader business context and how their work contributes to achieving organizational goals. By aligning third-party efforts with business objectives, organizations can ensure that the integration of AI technologies supports overall strategic priorities and delivers tangible business value.

- **Define Roles and Responsibilities:** Clearly articulate the roles and responsibilities of both the internal team and the third-party vendors. This clarity helps in managing expectations and ensures that all parties know what is expected of them in the AI integration process. Clearly defined roles and responsibilities prevent overlap, confusion, and potential conflicts, enabling smoother collaboration and more efficient project execution. It also helps in accountability, ensuring that each team knows their specific duties and the importance of their contributions to the overall success of AI initiatives.

- **Evaluate Performance:** Implement monitoring mechanisms to regularly assess the performance of third-party providers. This includes evaluating their contribution to IT maturity in the context of AI integration and adjusting as needed. Regular performance evaluations are critical for identifying strengths and areas for improvement, ensuring that third-party efforts continuously meet the organization's standards and expectations. Performance metrics and assessments provide valuable insights that can inform decision-making and strategic adjustments, ultimately enhancing the effectiveness of AI integration efforts.

- **Knowledge Transfer and Training:** Encourage knowledge sharing between the internal IT team and third-party providers. Effective knowledge transfer is essential for building a competent and cohesive team capable of leveraging AI technologies. This can be facilitated through joint training sessions, workshops, and regular knowledge exchange meetings. By promoting continuous learning and skill development, organizations can ensure that both internal and external teams are equipped with the latest knowledge and best practices in AI, fostering innovation and improving overall project outcomes.

- **Risk Management and Compliance:** Ensure that third-party providers adhere to the organization's standards for risk management and compliance, especially in areas critical to AI, such as data security, privacy, and ethical considerations. Effective risk management and compliance are crucial for protecting the organization from potential threats and ensuring the ethical and responsible use of AI technologies. This involves regular audits, adherence to regulatory requirements, and the implementation of robust risk mitigation strategies to safeguard the organization's interests and maintain trust.

- **Flexibility in Contracts and Agreements:** Advocate for flexibility in contracts with third-party providers to allow for adjustments as the organization's AI needs evolve. This includes provisions for scaling up or down and adapting to new technologies or methodologies. Flexible contracts enable organizations to respond quickly to changes in the technological landscape, ensuring that they can take advantage of new opportunities and innovations. By incorporating flexibility into agreements, organizations can maintain agility and resilience in their AI initiatives, driving long-term success and adaptability.

Rapidly Evolving AI Technologies

The AI technology landscape is evolving at a breakneck pace. This rapid evolution can challenge IT departments to keep up with the latest advancements, integrate them into the existing IT infrastructure, and ensure that the staff is trained on new technologies. A leader can mitigate this challenge through several strategic approaches:

- **Continuous Learning and Development:** Foster a culture of continuous learning within the IT department. Encourage and facilitate regular training, workshops, and knowledge-sharing sessions to keep the team updated with the latest AI technologies. This could include subscriptions to online courses, attending industry conferences, or partnerships with academic institutions. By promoting continuous learning, IT departments can ensure that their staff remains proficient in the latest AI tools and methodologies, enhancing their ability to innovate and adapt to new technological advancements.

- **Collaboration With Vendors and AI Communities:** Build strong relationships with AI technology vendors and participate in AI communities and forums. Vendors often offer training resources as part of their services, many times for free or as value-added services. Engaging with vendors and AI communities can provide insights into emerging trends and best practices, and offer early access to new tools and technologies. These relationships can also foster a network of support and collaboration, enabling IT departments to leverage external expertise and resources effectively.

- **Innovation Labs and Sandboxes:** Establish innovation labs or dedicate resources to exploring new AI technologies. This can be a sandbox environment where IT staff can experiment with new technologies without the pressure of immediate integration into the main IT infrastructure. Innovation labs provide a safe space for creativity and experimentation, allowing teams to test and refine AI solutions before deployment. This approach encourages a culture of innovation and continuous improvement, driving the organization's AI capabilities forward.

- **Knowledge Management Systems:** Implement knowledge management systems to capture and share learnings and best practices about new AI technologies. Knowledge management systems ensure that valuable insights and experiences are retained and accessible to the entire IT team. By creating a centralized repository of knowledge, organizations can streamline the dissemination of information, reduce redundancy, and promote a culture of shared learning and collaboration.

- **Partnerships:** Form strategic partnerships with academic institutions, research organizations, and technology consortia. These partnerships can provide access to cutting-edge research, talent, and tools in the AI space. Collaborating with academic and research institutions can also offer opportunities for joint projects, internships, and talent acquisition, enhancing the organization's capacity to innovate and stay ahead of technological trends.

- **Agile and Flexible IT Strategies:** Promote IT strategies that are inherently agile and adaptable. This allows for quicker adjustments to new technologies and methodologies. Encourage a mindset where change and adaptation are expected and planned for, rather than seen as disruptions. By fostering an agile environment, IT departments can respond swiftly to technological advancements, market changes, and emerging opportunities, ensuring that the organization remains competitive and resilient in the face of rapid technological evolution.

Resistance to Change

Resistance from IT employees and management can hinder the adoption of AI. This includes skepticism about AI's effectiveness, concerns over job displacement, and discomfort with new technologies and processes. Resistance to change, particularly in the context of AI adoption, is a common challenge in organizations. A leader can mitigate this challenge through several focused strategies:

- **Change Advocacy and Leadership Buy-In:** Secure and showcase strong support from leadership. Leaders should act as advocates for change, demonstrating their commitment to AI initiatives. Their active involvement can significantly influence the organization's attitude towards AI.

- **Manage Expectations:** Set realistic expectations about what AI can and cannot do. Over-hyping AI capabilities can lead to disappointment and increased resistance if the technology fails to deliver as promised.

- **Effective Communication on the Role of AI in IT:** Open, transparent, and continuous communication is crucial. Clearly articulate the benefits of AI, how it can augment human work, and the positive impact it can have on the organization. Address concerns directly and provide facts to dispel myths and misinformation about AI.

- **Inclusive Participation and Feedback:** Involve IT employees in the AI adoption process. Seek their input and feedback during various stages, from planning to implementation. This inclusion helps in making them feel valued and reduces resistance as they have a say in the process.

- **Training and Education:** Offer comprehensive training programs to upskill employees in relevant AI technologies. Understanding how AI works and how it can be a tool for efficiency and job enhancement reduces fear and builds confidence.

- **Showcase Early Successes:** Sharing these successes can build confidence in the technology and its applications, helping to overcome skepticism and resistance.

- **Create a Supportive Culture:** Foster a culture that is open to experimentation and learning. Encourage a mindset where trying new things and sometimes failing is considered part of the journey towards innovation.

- **Peer Champions and Change Agents:** Identify and empower change champions within the IT department. These are individuals who are enthusiastic about AI and can influence their peers positively.

What's Next?

As organizations embark on the journey of integrating Generative AI into their operations, it is essential to recognize the diverse perspectives that shape the workforce's response to this transformative technology. The Optimists, Pragmatists, and the Concerned each bring valuable insights to the table, highlighting the potential benefits, challenges, and risks associated with AI adoption. To successfully navigate this complex landscape, leaders must strike a delicate balance between harnessing AI's potential for growth and innovation while addressing the concerns and apprehensions of their employees.

By understanding and acknowledging these differing viewpoints, organizations can develop a comprehensive approach to workplace readiness that encompasses training, organizational point of view, culture, roles, and talent management. Through strategic planning, effective communication, and a commitment to ethical and responsible AI integration, leaders can guide their organizations towards a future where the power of Generative AI is fully realized, fostering a collaborative and thriving workplace environment, Our next chapter, "Part IV: Cultivating an Aligned, AI-Ready Workforce" focuses on this entirely so that leaders can embrace and leverage AI effectively.

YOU'RE
DOING
GREAT

Part IV: Cultivating an Aligned, AI-Ready Workforce

The idea of integrating GenAI into the workplace has generated a range of opinions. These views can be broadly classified into three groups: Optimists, Pragmatists, and the Concerned. These perspectives provide a nuanced understanding of how AI is transforming our work environments and the speed at which it should be adopted.

The Optimists: Enthusiasts of Innovation

Optimists herald AI as a revolutionary force destined to spark innovation, enhance efficiency, and unlock new opportunities that demand immediate exploration and implementation. They perceive AI not merely as a tool but as a powerful ally that augments human capabilities, boosting productivity and fostering creativity across diverse sectors. This group is composed of visionaries who envisage a future where AI transcends the automation of mundane tasks, ushering in novel job roles and entirely new industries. They are exhilarated by AI's potential as a co-creator, anticipating a future where the technology catalyzes more job creation than displacement by uncovering needs and opportunities previously unimagined.

For the optimists, the promise of AI aligns with the vision of a brighter, more prosperous working world. They champion the belief that, when harnessed responsibly, AI can revolutionize the workplace, driving substantial improvements in efficiency and opening the door to unprecedented opportunities for growth and innovation.

The Pragmatists: Advocates for Synergistic Balance

Pragmatists in the workplace adopt a balanced perspective on AI integration. They acknowledge AI's transformative potential but also recognize its limitations. This group places high value on indispensable human skills such as empathy, critical thinking, and creative problem-solving, which AI cannot replicate.

Pragmatists champion a collaborative ecosystem where AI tools and human intelligence complement each other, leveraging their unique strengths. They emphasize that while AI will undoubtedly redefine the nature of work, it is crucial to maintain a human-centric approach. Pragmatists view AI as a tool that, when used judiciously, can enhance job satisfaction and productivity by automating routine tasks, thereby freeing up humans to engage in more complex and fulfilling work.

This group advocates for a measured approach to AI adoption. They stress the importance of adaptability and continuous learning to navigate the evolving job market. Pragmatists are methodical in assessing AI's impact and pace of integration, ensuring that the technology is implemented thoughtfully and responsibly, with a focus on long-term benefits and sustainability.

The Concerned: Prioritizing AI's Challenges and Risks

The concerned group voices significant apprehensions regarding the swift integration of AI into the workforce. Their worries revolve around several critical issues:

- **Job Displacement:** There is a palpable fear that AI could replace human workers, leading to widespread unemployment and economic instability.
- **Ethical Implications:** Concerns about the ethical use of AI, including issues related to privacy, bias, and decision-making transparency, are at the forefront.

- **Societal Impact:** This group is wary of the broader societal consequences, such as widening economic inequality. They fear that AI might disproportionately benefit those with advanced skills, thereby exacerbating the divide between different workforce segments.

However, the perspective of the Concerned is not merely rooted in skepticism; it is a call for cautious, deliberate, and responsible AI integration. They advocate for:

- **Strong Ethical Guidelines:** Establishing robust frameworks to govern AI usage ethically.

- **Transparency:** Ensuring transparency in AI operations and decision-making processes to build trust and accountability.

- **Equitable Access to AI Education and Opportunities:** Providing widespread access to AI-related education and skill development to ensure inclusivity.

The Concerned stress the importance of preparing the workforce for an AI-driven future through comprehensive education and targeted training programs. Their viewpoint is essential in framing AI adoption in a manner that is inclusive, ethical, and mindful of its broader societal implications.

Each perspective—Optimists, Pragmatists, and the Concerned—offers valuable insights, collectively contributing to a holistic understanding of AI's evolving role in the workplace. Leaders must understand how these beliefs are distributed throughout the organization and be prepared to address them as GenAI technology proliferates. The key to navigating this complex landscape lies in striking a balance: leveraging AI's potential for growth and innovation while addressing its inherent challenges to ensure its benefits are accessible and equitable for all.

This is the approach used in developing the graphic below.

CATEGORY	COMPONENT	Proof of Concept (Experiments)	Quick Wins (Employee Tasks)	Changes (Single Department Processes)	Cross Functional (Multi-Department Processes)	Transformational (New Business)
WORKFORCE	Training	●	●	●	●	●
	Organizational Point of View		●	●	●	●
	Culture		●	●	●	●
	Roles		●	●	●	●
	Talent Management			●	●	●

CHANGE COMPLEXITY & RISK →

Training

Training programs are essential for enhancing the knowledge and skills of employees regarding AI technologies. These initiatives should cover fundamental AI concepts, provide a basic understanding of GenAI, and explore its applications, tools, and implications for work processes. Effective training ensures employees are well-prepared to leverage AI in their daily tasks.

Organizational Point of View

An organization's perspective on AI encompasses its vision, policies, and strategic approach to AI integration. Steering Leadership should define this view early, establishing "guard rails" that align AI adoption with the organization's broader culture and values.

Culture

Fostering an AI-positive culture involves cultivating shared values, beliefs, and practices that promote AI innovation and adaptation. This culture should align with the organization's overall ethos and encourage employees to embrace AI technologies.

Roles

Redefining roles and responsibilities is crucial as AI integrates into organizational processes. This includes redesigning job roles based on task automation, updating performance goals, and considering organizational design adjustments. Human Resources is a key partner in managing these changes.

Talent Management

Talent management is vital for AI readiness. It involves identifying, recruiting, developing, and retaining individuals with the necessary skills for AI-related tasks. Aligning human resource strategies with AI initiatives ensures the organization can thrive in an AI-driven landscape.

Let's look at how leaders can facilitate Workplace Readiness in a balanced way for these groups.

Training

In this section, we outline the training continuity based on an organization's progression through various project types—acknowledging the increase in change complexity and risk.

Proof of Concept (Experiments)

During Proof of Concept phases, training should start with content from the Governance and Technology categories. This foundation ensures that PoCs are executed safely and compliantly, accelerating the time to value determination for the organization. While training in the use of specific tools (e.g., prompting, navigation) is necessary, it may not need to be formalized.

Important Considerations for Leaders

Tailor training to address the specific needs of different individuals:

- **Optimists:** Engage their enthusiasm for innovation by focusing on cutting-edge aspects of AI. Include advanced topics on potential breakthroughs and encourage creative thinking about AI applications.

- **Pragmatists:** Offer practical, hands-on experimentation while emphasizing AI's realistic limitations and current capabilities. This balance helps them understand both the potential and the boundaries of AI.

- **Concerned:** Address ethical considerations and responsible AI use upfront. Include discussions on potential impacts and safeguards to ensure they see these experiments as thoughtful and conscientious.

Quick Wins (Employee Tasks)

As PoCs prove valuable and begin to be productionalized, the workforce will become more aware of the organization's intent to use GenAI. This shift signifies a commitment to GenAI. To ensure alignment across all functions, formal training on Governance will be critical enterprise-wide and may become required due to legal or compliance needs.

Important Considerations for Leaders

Align with Steering Leadership on an organization-wide training approach for Governance readiness, including Ethical and Responsible Use and Legal aspects. Consider enterprise-wide training on Technology readiness (e.g., data and architectural topics) for non-technical people. This training may be incorporated into business compliance and new hire training.

- **Optimists:** Highlight how AI tools can lead to significant efficiency gains and open new avenues for creative problem-solving.

- **Pragmatists:** Focus on the immediate benefits of AI in improving task efficiency. Demonstrate how AI can free up time for more complex and rewarding work, aligning with their human-centric approach.

- **Concerned:** Ensure training includes robust information on the complementary nature of AI. Emphasize AI's role in aiding human workers.

Changes (Single Department Processes)

These projects focus on enhancing and/or automating workflows within single departments. The organization should now be more aware of GenAI use.

Important Considerations for Leaders

Ensure that Governance readiness training is widely available. If not, continue to proliferate it but ensure stakeholders impacted by these initiatives receive it as prerequisites.

- **Optimists:** Foster interest in departmental transformation through AI. Showcase how AI can streamline processes and lead to innovative departmental practices.

- **Pragmatists:** Offer in-depth training on how AI impacts processes and best practices. Include case studies showing successful AI integration in similar settings, aligning with their methodical approach.

- **Concerned:** Provide reassurances on maintaining the human element. Focus on training that highlights increased departmental efficiency and effectiveness without compromising human values.

Cross-Functional (Multi-Department Processes)

Cross-functional initiatives link departmental processes into large organizational domains, such as Customer Experience Management or Enterprise Risk Management.

Important Considerations for Leaders

By this stage, the organization should be fully aware of GenAI's use and context. Governance readiness training should be widely available.

- **Optimists:** Encourage exploration of AI in facilitating cross-departmental collaboration and innovation. Show the big picture of organizational transformation.

- **Pragmatists:** Emphasize AI's synergistic potential in enhancing cross-functional communication and cooperation. Training should illustrate how AI serves as a bridge between departments.

- **Concerned:** Address concerns about AI's broader implications across departments. Ensure transparency in AI usage and its impact on the workforce, highlighting collaborative benefits and ethical considerations.

Transformational (New Business)

Transformational initiatives involve radical innovations for new AI-driven business models and capabilities.

Important Considerations for Leaders

Focus on growth, emphasizing innovation, business models, and GenAI applications. Tailor training to:

- **Optimists:** Capitalize on their forward-thinking nature by exploring new business models and strategic AI applications. Discuss AI as a catalyst for business innovation and growth.

- **Pragmatists:** Provide extensive training on integrating AI into strategic planning and decision-making. Show practical steps to adapt to new business models driven by AI.

- **Concerned:** Address potential societal impacts and ethical implications of AI-driven business transformation. Include modules on sustainable and equitable AI practices, ensuring they see the transition as responsible and inclusive.

By tailoring the training approach to each project type and considering the perspectives of these three groups, organizations can foster harmonious and effective AI integration in the workplace. This strategy ensures that everyone, regardless of their initial stance on AI, is equipped with the knowledge and skills to adapt to the evolving AI landscape.

Organizational Point of View

The significance of establishing a clear organizational point of view on AI integration cannot be overstated. As the workforce embarks on the Organization's AI journey, diverse perspectives will naturally emerge. It is essential for Steering Leadership to define a coherent strategy, acting as "guard rails" to guide the evolution of the organization's culture in relation to Generative AI. This strategy should encompass the organization's vision, policies, and strategic approach to seamlessly integrating and leveraging AI within its operations, grounded in the outcomes of Governance Readiness. Crucially, this point of view must include leadership's perspective on the impacts of AI on its workforce.

Trust in leadership is pivotal in addressing employee concerns about the integration of GenAI in the workplace. As GenAI transforms business operations, employee apprehensions—such as job security, ethical use, and the implications of AI on their roles—will inevitably rise. Leaders who have established a foundation of trust can more effectively navigate these concerns. Trusted leaders are more likely to see employees engage constructively in the transition process, participate in training programs, and adapt to new ways of working. Delaying the address of employees' rising concerns can erode trust, making the transition more challenging.

The optimal time to develop and communicate this organizational point of view is after the completion of several Proof of Concepts and a couple of Quick Wins. This timing will help mitigate potential rumors and energize future efforts.

Important Considerations for Leaders

Below is a template that leaders can adapt:

- **Acknowledgment of Diverse Perspectives:** Start by acknowledging the varying viewpoints within the organization, emphasizing that each perspective is valuable and contributes to a well-rounded approach to AI integration. Highlight the positives of each perspective—whether optimistic, pragmatic, or concerned.

- **Future-Focused Vision:** Share a vision of a future where AI leads to a more prosperous, efficient, and fulfilling working environment. Emphasize how this benefits the organization, its employees, and the broader society, including a stance on corporate citizenship.

- **Commitment to Innovation and Efficiency:** Stress the organization's dedication to leveraging AI for innovation and efficiency. Highlight the creation of new opportunities and enhanced productivity, sharing progress, successes, and learnings from GenAI initiatives.

- **Importance of Ethical and Responsible AI Application:** Address concerns by committing to ethical AI practices, including transparency, fairness, and responsible use of AI. Ensure these practices align with the organization's values and societal norms.

- **AI as a Complement to Human Skills:** Emphasize that AI is a tool designed to augment human talent, creating new roles and opportunities. Highlight AI's role in automating mundane tasks, allowing employees to focus on creative and complex work that demands human ingenuity. Discuss the value of a synergistic relationship where AI and human intelligence work together, each playing to their strengths for better outcomes.

- **Commitment to Equitable Opportunities:** Promise to provide equal access to AI-related education and opportunities, ensuring all employees, regardless of their current skill level, can benefit from AI advancements.

- **Investment in Continuous Learning:** Recognize the importance of ongoing education and skill development. Assure employees that the company will invest in training programs to help them adapt to and thrive in an AI-enhanced workplace.

- **Open Communication and Inclusivity:** Create opportunities for employees to engage with the organization's point of view on GenAI. Encourage feedback and consider concerns from all employees, fostering a culture of inclusivity and open communication.

By addressing these considerations, leaders can effectively manage the integration of GenAI, ensuring a smooth transition that aligns with the organization's strategic goals and values while maintaining employee trust and engagement.

AI Positive Culture

Understanding and shaping organizational culture can often be a complex and elusive endeavor. This section is designed to assist leaders in preparing their organizations to adopt and integrate Generative AI technologies, without necessarily overhauling the existing cultural framework. Rather than reinvesting the culture entirely—whether it is viewed positively or negatively—this approach focuses on embedding a perspective on GenAI within the existing cultural landscape.

Organizational culture in the context of AI adoption encompasses the collective values, beliefs, and practices that shape how members of an organization perceive, interact with, and leverage AI technologies. The goal is to cultivate an environment that supports AI innovation and smooth adaptation. As previously mentioned, an Organizational Point of View serves as the catalyst for this cultural evolution.

Important Considerations for Leaders

Building an AI-positive culture requires a multifaceted strategy. Below are some recommendations structured around the different stages of GenAI initiatives, beginning with Quick Wins and aligned with the sample Organizational Point of View provided earlier:

- **Quick Wins (Employee Tasks)**
    - **Highlight Immediate Benefits:** Clearly communicate how GenAI can streamline and enhance daily tasks, focusing on practical benefits to secure buy-in from employees. Highlight specific examples where AI can save time or improve task quality to make the advantages tangible.

   - **Provide Accessible Training:** Offer training sessions that are easy to understand and readily accessible. This will help employees quickly adapt to the new tools, alleviating any anxiety related to the use of new technology. Consider a mix of workshops, online tutorials, and hands-on practice sessions.

   - **Celebrate Early Adopters:** Recognize and reward employees who effectively integrate AI into their tasks. These early adopters can serve as role models and ambassadors, setting a positive example for their peers.

- **Changes (Single Department Processes)**

   - **Engage Department Leaders:** Collaborate with department heads to create AI champions who can drive change from within their teams. These leaders can help tailor AI implementations to meet specific departmental needs.

   - **Integrate AI Into Departmental Goals:** Align AI initiatives with the specific goals and objectives of each department to ensure that the technology feels relevant and purposeful. This alignment can also help in tracking the impact of AI on departmental performance.

   - **Facilitate Cross-Departmental Learning:** Encourage departments to share their AI experiences and best practices. This can be done through workshops, interdepartmental meetings, and knowledge-sharing platforms.

- **Cross-Functional (Multi-Department Processes)**
    - **Promote Interdepartmental Collaboration:** Establish forums and platforms where different departments can discuss AI integration, share insights, and collaborate on projects. This fosters a culture of cooperation and collective problem-solving.
    - **Customize Communication:** Tailor the messaging about AI to address the specific needs, concerns, and expectations of each department. Personalized communication can help in building trust and reducing resistance.
    - **Build a Community of Practice:** Create a community where employees from various departments can share knowledge, collaborate on AI-related projects, and support each other. This community can serve as a resource hub and innovation incubator.
- **Transformational (New Business)**
    - **Leadership Commitment and Vision:** Ensure that top leadership visibly supports and advocates for AI, embedding its importance into the organization's core values and vision. Leadership commitment is crucial in driving cultural change.

- **Foster a Culture of Innovation:** Encourage a mindset shift towards continuous innovation, where AI is seen as a key driver of growth and competitive advantage. Promote an experimental approach and celebrate innovative ideas and projects.
- **Manage Change Comprehensively:** Implement thorough change management practices that address not just technological adoption but also the cultural and behavioral shifts required to maximize the value of the new AI-driven venture. This includes clear communication, ongoing training, and support systems to help employees navigate the transition.

Roles in the Age of GenAI

As Generative AI technologies become increasingly integrated into organizational processes, it is imperative to thoroughly understand and thoughtfully consider their impacts on job roles and responsibilities. This integration necessitates a strategic reevaluation of how work is accomplished and how employees contribute to the organization's success.

Important Considerations for Leaders

While some may view the integration of AI with concern, it is crucial to recognize the potential of AI as a tool to augment human talent. This perspective opens up opportunities for creating new roles and enhancing existing ones. As organizations begin to implement GenAI solutions, starting with Quick Wins, it is essential to engage with Human Resources (HR) to review and anticipate how workforce impacts may evolve over time. Topics to address include:

- **Shifting Job Roles:** For some roles, the introduction of AI will mean a shift from manual or routine tasks to more strategic, analytical, or creative work. HR, in collaboration with department heads, must be prepared to identify these shifts and guide employees through the transition, ensuring they have the necessary training and support.

- **Redefining Performance Goals:** With AI taking over certain functions, performance metrics and expectations need to align with the new work dynamics. This might include placing a greater emphasis on outcomes like innovation, problem-solving, and collaboration, rather than traditional productivity measures.

- **Impact on Compensation:** As roles evolve, compensation structures may need to be adjusted to reflect the new responsibilities and skills required.

Human Resources

Human Resources plays a pivotal role in this transformation. They are key partners to leaders in managing the human aspect of AI integration.

Important Considerations for Leaders

There are now several studies available that investigated the impacts of GenAI on productivity, beginning in 2023. More and more are published every day. Leaders should stay abreast of the evolving research.

Below are recommendations for leaders to consider in working with Human Resources through the continuity of AI Projects:

Quick Wins (Employee Tasks)

- **Identify Impact Areas:** Work with HR to pinpoint specific tasks within roles that can be enhanced or replaced by AI, focusing on immediate efficiency gains.

- **Role Adjustment:** Collaborate on adjusting job descriptions as needed to reflect new responsibilities and the integration of AI tools.

- **Performance Metrics Revision:** Redefine performance goals to align with the enhanced capabilities provided by AI.

- **Training and Support:** Ensure that the necessary training and support for employees adapting to new tools and responsibilities is planned and available.

Changes (Single Department Processes)

- **Departmental Role Analysis:** Conduct an in-depth analysis of how AI will change workflows and roles within the affected department.

- **Collaborative Redesign:** Work with HR to redesign roles and responsibilities to align with the new departmental processes influenced by AI.

- **Career Pathing:** Assist HR in developing new career paths and opportunities for growth within the transformed department.

- **Change Communication:** Coordinate with HR to effectively communicate these role changes and their benefits to employees.

Cross-Functional (Multi-Department Processes)

- **Interdepartmental Collaboration:** Facilitate cross-departmental discussions with HR to understand the broader impact of AI on roles across the organization.

- **Unified Role Redefinition:** Ensure consistency in role redefinition across departments based upon previous work.

- **Cross-Training Programs:** Develop cross-training programs with HR to enhance understanding across departments, collaboration, and potential opportunities.

- **Culture and Engagement:** Work with HR to foster a culture that embraces cross-functional collaboration and adaptability.

Transformational (New Business)

- **Strategic Workforce Planning:** Partner with HR in strategic workforce planning to align human capital with the new business direction.
- **Comprehensive Role Redesign:** Engage in an organization-wide role redesign, considering the implications of AI on all levels and functions affected.
- **Leadership Development:** Focus on leadership development programs to guide the organization through the transformation.

Talent Management

Talent management is intrinsically linked with the evolution of roles within an organization as it adopts AI technologies. As HR departments begin to implement organizational design principles in response to AI integration, their focus shifts to ensuring that the organization has the right talent in place to support this transformation. This involves a comprehensive approach to managing the workforce, aligning talent strategies closely with AI initiatives.

Important Considerations for Leaders

Talent management is a core competency of HR. Once the Leader has engaged HR for Roles Readiness, HR can incorporate GenAI impacts into their talent management processes. For awareness, leaders can refer to the list below on possible actions HR may take:

- **Recruiting AI-Savvy Talent:** HR must adapt its recruitment strategies to attract individuals who are proficient in AI skills or show a strong potential to excel in this domain.

- **Developing Existing Employees:** As AI transforms existing roles, there's a significant need to develop current employees to meet new demands. This involves providing training and development opportunities, including workshops, online courses, certification programs, or advanced education opportunities.

- **Retention Strategies:** Retaining talent is equally important in the era of AI. HR must develop retention strategies that recognize and reward AI expertise and contributions, which could involve career development paths, competitive compensation packages, and opportunities for innovative work.

- **Cultural Fit and Adaptation:** Beyond technical skills, it's essential to consider how individuals fit into the company's culture and adapt to changes brought by AI. This involves evaluating and nurturing skills like adaptability, problem-solving, and teamwork, which are crucial in a rapidly evolving AI landscape.

What's Next?

As we conclude our discussion on cultivating an AI-ready workforce, we look ahead to building an actionable strategy.

Next, we'll dive into "Part V: Developing Your Own Organization's Playbook to Organizational Readiness for Generative AI." This section will guide you through identifying GenAI initiatives, assessing organizational readiness and risks, and charting your next steps.

We'll also cover how to draft a roadmap of activities and integrate it into your strategy, ensuring your organization is prepared for AI-driven transformation.

Do it Together
Never Alone

Part V:
Developing Your Own Organization's Playbook to Organizational Readiness for Generative AI

Reviewing GenAI Project Types

This guide has explored the dynamic world of Organizational Readiness for Generative AI. As we conclude, you should consolidate your learnings into a strategic playbook.

The landscape of GenAI projects can be broad, encompassing everything from small, exploratory experiments to large-scale, transformative initiatives. Therefore, it's vital to systematically catalog these projects to ensure a comprehensive view of how GenAI is being leveraged and where its potential lies.

Here's a breakdown of the types of GenAI projects you might encounter. Even though we have discussed these projects in detail it is still recommended to review the below provided comparisons as a leader of your organization.

1. **Proof of Concept Projects**

    - **Description:** PoC projects in AI are exploratory and experimental endeavors designed to test the feasibility and potential impact of GenAI technologies in a controlled environment. These small-scale projects often serve as the initial step towards broader AI adoption.

- **Examples:** You might find PoC projects that utilize AI to automate simple, repetitive tasks or to analyze specific datasets. The aim here is to validate whether the AI solution can effectively solve the problem at hand.

2. **Quick Wins (Employee Tasks)**

   - **Description:** Quick wins involve deploying GenAI solutions to enhance specific, often manual, employee tasks. These projects aim to streamline workflows, increase efficiency, and deliver immediate value to the organization.

   - **Examples:** Implementing ChatGPT for drafting emails or reports, using AI tools for data entry, or employing AI-driven scheduling assistants are all examples of quick-win projects.

3. **Process Changes (Single Department Processes)**

   - **Description:** This category involves the implementation of GenAI technologies to transform processes within a single department. These initiatives aim to improve the efficiency and effectiveness of departmental operations.

   - **Examples:** Deploying AI chatbots in customer service departments, using AI for predictive maintenance in manufacturing, or employing AI-driven analytics for marketing campaigns.

4. **Cross-Functional Projects (Multi-Department Processes)**

   - **Description:** Cross-functional projects have a broader scope, impacting end-to-end processes across multiple departments. These initiatives often require coordination among various teams and can significantly enhance the overall efficiency of organizational operations.

   - **Examples:** AI-driven supply chain optimization, integrating AI in enterprise resource planning (ERP) systems, or using AI for cross-departmental data analysis and insights.

5. **Transformational Initiatives (New Business Models or Capabilities)**

   - **Description:** These are large-scale, transformative projects that redefine business models or create entirely new lines of business.

Transformational initiatives leverage GenAI to drive innovation and create competitive advantages.

- **Examples:** Entering new markets with AI-powered products, developing new services like AI-driven health diagnostics, or creating innovative customer experiences through AI personalization.

Identify the GenAI Initiatives in Your Organization

To effectively identify and categorize your GenAI initiatives, consider constructing a comprehensive inventory. This inventory should include detailed descriptions of each project, its current status, objectives, involved stakeholders, and potential impact on the organization.

Here's an example of how to structure this inventory:

Type of AI Project	Description	My Organization's Initiatives
Proof of Concept	PoC projects in AI are experimental endeavors exploring the potential of GenAI technologies. Typically, these are small-scale projects validating the feasibility and effectiveness of AI solutions in a controlled environment.	[List your initiatives here]
Quick Wins (Employee Tasks)	Implementation of GenAI solutions to enhance specific employee tasks, like using ChatGPT for draft copywriting. Aims to streamline workflows and increase efficiency in targeted areas.	[List your initiatives here]

Continued on next page…

Type of AI Project	Description	My Organization's Initiatives
Process Changes (Single Department Processes)	Implementing GenAI to transform processes within a single department, like deploying chatbots in customer service. Aims to enhance departmental efficiency and effectiveness.	[List your initiatives here]
Cross-Functional Projects (Multi-Department Processes)	Broader scope projects impacting end-to-end processes across multiple departments, like AI-driven supply chain optimization.	[List your initiatives here]
Transformational Initiatives (New Business Models or Capabilities)	Projects that create new lines of business or capabilities, like entering music production in a book publishing business.	[List your initiatives here]

Readiness Assessment

To help you systematically evaluate your organization's readiness, reference the Gen AI Organizational Model and the subsequent table below in the following activity:

CATEGORY	COMPONENT	Proof of Concept (Experiments)	Quick Wins (Employee Tasks)	Changes (Single Department Processes)	Cross Functional (Multi-Department Processes)	Transformational (New Business)
GOVERNANCE	Steering Leadership	●	●	●	●	●
	Ethics & Responsible Use	●	●	●	●	●
	Legal	●	●	●	●	●
	Usage		●	●	●	●
TECHNOLOGY	Data	●	●	●	●	●
	Architecture	●	●	●	●	●
	Security	●	●	●	●	●
	Vendor Standards	●	●	●	●	●
	IT Maturity				●	●
WORKFORCE	Training	●	●	●	●	●
	Organizational Point of View		●	●	●	●
	Culture		●	●	●	●
	Roles		●	●	●	●
	Talent Management			●	●	●

CHANGE COMPLEXITY & RISK →

Category	Component	Action Required
Governance	Steering Leadership	Develop clear leadership strategies and responsibilities
	Ethics and Responsible Use	Implement a code of ethics and responsible use policies
	Legal	Ensure compliance with all relevant legal requirements
	Usage	Establish clear guidelines for data usage
Technology	Data	Improve data management and privacy practices
	Architecture	Update or redesign system architecture for efficiency
	Security	Enhance security measures

Category	Component	Action Required
	Vendor Standards	Establish and enforce vendor standards
	IT Maturity	Develop a roadmap for IT infrastructure improvement
Workplace	Training	Implement ongoing training programs
	Organizational Point of View	Foster a positive organizational perspective towards technology
	Culture	Encourage a culture of innovation and positivity
	Roles	Define clear roles and responsibilities within the organization
	Talent Management	Implement effective talent management strategies

Assess Potential Risks

Using your project inventory, identify risks and potential impacts associated with any readiness components that may be lacking or improperly timed relative to the projects you identified and the GenAI Organizational model. This involves:

- **Risk Identification:** Identifying gaps related to governance, technology, and workforce components in POCs, Quick Wins, Changes, etc.

- **Impact Analysis:** Determining the potential impact of these risks on your GenAI initiatives.

- **Prioritization:** Prioritizing risks based on their potential impact and likelihood.

Risk Assessment Table

Here's a table format to help in assessing risks with sample values:

Project Type / Project / Component	Identified Risks	Potential Impact
Quick Win / AI Image Creation / Legal	Non-compliance with regulations	Legal penalties and reputational damage
Quick Win / AI Image Creation / Data	Incomplete or poor-quality data	Ineffective AI models and results

Quick Win / AI Image Creation / Training	Lack of skilled personnel	Delayed project timelines and increased costs

Chart Your Next Steps for Organizational Readiness

With a clear understanding of your readiness and the components that need attention, you can now plan your next steps. This phase may involve:

- **Governance Enhancements:** Developing detailed plans to enhance governance frameworks, including updating policies and defining roles.
- **Technology Upgrades:** Supporting the upgrade of technology to ensure robust support for AI workloads.
- **Workforce Development:** Nurturing an AI-conducive culture through training programs and skill development initiatives.

Each step should align with your overall business strategy and contribute to closing the readiness gaps previously identified.

Action Plan Table

Use the table below with sample data to plan your next steps:

Project Type / Project / Component	Action Required	Responsible Party	Resources Needed	Timing
Quick Win / AI Image Creation / Legal	Include AI-specifics	Governance Team	Legal and compliance expertise	Now
Quick Win / AI Image Creation / Data	Enhance data practices	IT/Data Team	Data management tools and training	In 2 months
Quick Win / AI Image Creation / Training	Implement training programs	HR/Training Team	Training materials and budget	In 6 months

Drafting a Roadmap of Activities

Your GenAI readiness journey now requires a comprehensive roadmap. This document should:

- **Projects**
- **Detailed Activities:** List specific activities required to achieve readiness.
- **Timelines:** Outline the timelines for each activity.

- **Responsible Parties:** Specify who is responsible for each task.

- **Resources Required:** Identify the resources needed to execute each activity.

- **Milestones:** Set clear milestones to track progress.

The roadmap is a living document, evolving as your organization progresses in its GenAI journey and as the field of GenAI itself evolves. It should balance ambition with realism, pushing your organization forward while acknowledging the potential challenges you've identified.

Integrate Your Roadmap Into the Change Management Strategy

Organizational Readiness is a vital input for developing a comprehensive change management strategy. This ensures that GenAI initiatives are not isolated but are part of the broader narrative of organizational change and transformation. Integrating GenAI into your change management strategy involves:

- **Alignment:** Aligning GenAI goals with overall business objectives.

- **Stakeholder Engagement:** Ensuring stakeholder buy-in.

- **Impact Management:** Managing the impacts on employees and processes.

- **Continuous Learning:** Maintaining a focus on continuous learning and adaptation.

NOTHING IS
IMPOSSIBLE

Conclusion

As we conclude this comprehensive guide on preparing your organization for Generative AI, it is essential to recognize that this journey is far more than merely adopting new technology; it is a strategic transformation. Throughout this book, we've explored critical areas necessary for ensuring your organization's GenAI readiness, from understanding the organizational AI journey to fostering an AI-positive culture.

In **Part I**, we examined the foundational elements of embarking on the organizational AI journey. We addressed the importance of avoiding an "overly technology-led" approach, ensuring your strategy remains balanced and holistic.

In **Part II**, we delved into governance readiness, emphasizing the necessity of strong leadership, ethical considerations, legal frameworks, and responsible usage. Effective governance is the bedrock of sustainable AI success.

Part III highlighted the impact of AI technology architecture on change success. Critical components like data management, system architecture, security, vendor standards, and IT maturity were discussed to ensure your technological infrastructure supports your AI ambitions.

Part IV focused on cultivating an AI-ready workforce. Training, fostering an AI-positive culture, defining roles, and managing talent are vital to creating a team that can adapt and thrive in an AI-enhanced environment.

Finally, in **Part V**, we guided you through developing your organization's playbook for GenAI readiness. This included identifying GenAI initiatives, assessing organizational readiness and risks, and creating a detailed roadmap integrated into your change management strategy.

As you implement these strategies, remember that the GenAI landscape is continually evolving. Your approach must remain dynamic, informed, and resilient. Your role as a Leader is crucial; your vision, insight, and leadership will transform challenges into opportunities.

Embrace the journey ahead with an open mind and a proactive stance. Leverage the knowledge and tools provided, and continuously adapt to stay ahead. Your commitment to staying informed and agile will be the cornerstone of your organization's success in this new era of GenAI.

Thank you for entrusting this guide as your companion. Here's to your success in shaping a future filled with innovation, efficiency, and sustainable growth.

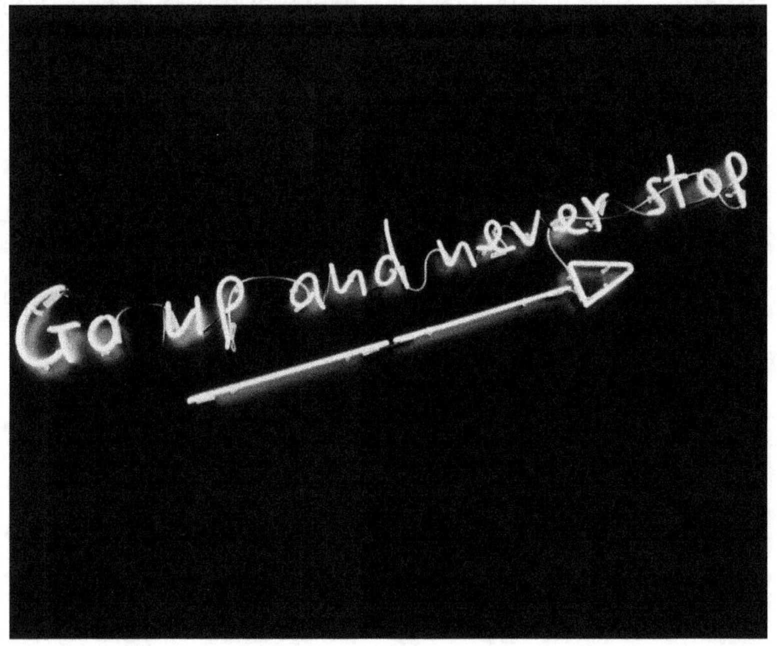
Go up and never stop

References

Acemoglu, D., & Johnson, S. (2023, October 25). *Choosing AI's impact on the future of work*. SSIR. https://ssir.org/articles/entry/ai-impact-on-jobs-and-work

Dzombak, R., & Palat, J. (2021, August 30). *5 ways to start growing an AI-ready workforce*. SEI Blog | Carnegie Mellon University. https://insights.sei.cmu.edu/blog/5-ways-to-start-growing-an-ai-ready-workforce/

Future trends: 5 ways AI will impact workers in 2024. (2023, November 21). The Career Success Blog. https://uvaro.com/blog/how-will-ai-impact-workers-in-2024

Georgieva, K. (2024, January 14). *AI will transform the global economy. Let's make sure it benefits humanity*. International Monetary Fund | IMF Blog https://www.imf.org/en/Blogs/Articles/2024/01/14/ai-will-transform-the-global-economy-lets-make-sure-it-benefits-humanity

Global banking practice: Building the AI bank of the future. (2021). McKinsey & Company. https://www.mckinsey.com/~/media/mckinsey/industries/financial%20services/our%20insights/building%20the%20ai%20bank%20of%20the%20future/building-the-ai-bank-of-the-future.pdf

Goldstein, J., Lobig, B., Fillare, C., & Nowak, C. (n.d.). *Augmented work for an automated, AI-driven world*. IBM.

https://www.ibm.com/thought-leadership/institute-business-value/en-us/report/augmented-workforce

Gurbacki, J. (2023, December 11). *AI's impact on tech workers and more: Predictions for 2024*. Broadleaf Results. broadleafresults.com/blog/trends/ais-impact-on-tech-workers-and-more-predictions-for-2024/

Howarth, J. (2024, March 27). *55+ new generative AI stats (2024)*. Exploding Topics. https://explodingtopics.com/blog/generative-ai-stats

Lieberman, A. (2023, September 5). *Strategies for scaling generative AI in large organizations*. Forbes. https://www.forbes.com/sites/forbestechcouncil/2023/09/05/strategies-for-scaling-generative-ai-in-large-organizations/?sh=51556b53b712

van der Meulen, R., & McCall, T. (2018, February 13). *Gartner says nearly half of CIOs are planning to deploy artificial intelligence*. Gartner. https://www.gartner.com/en/newsroom/press-releases/2018-02-13-gartner-says-nearly-half-of-cios-are-planning-to-deploy-artificial-intelligence

Ng, M. (2024, January 17). *Tech policy trends 2024: Generative AI's impact on the workforce*. Access Partnership. https://accesspartnership.com/tech-policy-trends-2024-generative-ais-impact-on-the-workforce/

Novartis and Microsoft announce collaboration to transform medicine with artificial intelligence. (2019, October 10). Novartis. https://www.novartis.com/news/novartis-and-microsoft-announce-collaboration-transform-medicine-artificial-intelligence

Ortiz, S. (2023, August 18). *40% of workers will have to reskill in the next three years due to AI, says IBM study*. ZDNET. https://www.zdnet.com/article/40-of-workers-will-have-to-reskill-in-the-next-three-years-due-to-ai-says-ibm-study/

Shook, E., & Daugherty, P. (2024, January 16). *Work, workforce, workers: Reinvented in the age of generative AI*. Accenture. https://www.accenture.com/us-en/insights/consulting/gen-ai-talent

Teare, G. (2024, June 5). *Crunchbase monthly recap May 2024: AI leads alongside an uptick in billion-dollar rounds*. Crunchbase News. https://news.crunchbase.com/venture/monthly-funding-recap-may-2024/

Zabinski, J. & Goodbaum, B. (2023, December 18). *University students explore AI's potential impact on the workforce*. American National Standards Institute - ANSI. https://www.ansi.org/standards-news/all-news/2023/12/12-18-23-university-students-explore-ais-potential-impact-on-the-workforce

Image References

Anna. (2019, September 29). *Dream brig neon signage* [Image]. Unsplash. https://unsplash.com/photos/dream-brig-neon-signage-B6k7v0eIOYo

Beamer, D. (2018a, November 18). *Habits to be made LED signage* [Image]. Unsplash. https://unsplash.com/photos/habits-to-be-made-led-signage-uejtDqpJ7ig

Billingsey, C. (2019, July 7). *Red neon signage* [Image]. Unsplash. https://unsplash.com/photos/red-neon-signage-PQ36AkKJfAc

Harvey, S. (2017, December 2). *I am bold neon signage at night time* [Image]. Unsplash. https://unsplash.com/photos/i-am-bold-neon-signage-at-night-time-SoZ3b8LLOdo

Jarrett, A. (2021, January 20). *Text* [Image]. Unsplash. https://unsplash.com/photos/text-aOm1qcNc6Lw

Tyson, J. (2019, November 1). *Red you're doing great neon sign* [Image]. Unsplash. https://unsplash.com/photos/red-youred-doing-great-neon-sign-OZz8TK8T8MM

Zaric, M. (2019, September 5). *Nothing is impossible signage* [Image]. Unsplash. https://unsplash.com/photos/nothing-is-impossible-signage-QMwkGYFDjiE

www.ingramcontent.com/pod-product-compliance
Lightning Source LLC
LaVergne TN
LVHW051234050326
832903LV00028B/2398
* 9 7 9 8 3 2 9 2 5 1 3 3 3 *